MINDSET
MATTERS

MINDSET MATTERS

THE CORRECT CRAFT WAY

BILL YEARGIN | ZACH HUTCHESON

Published in the United States by
Ignite Press
55 Shaw Ave. #204
Clovis, CA 93612
www.IgnitePress.us

ISBN: 979-8-9851202-7-1
ISBN: 979-8-9851202-8-8 (Hardcover)
ISBN: 979-8-9851202-9-5 (E-book)

For bulk purchases, contact:

Correct Craft
7500 Amsterdam Dr
Orlando, FL 32832
689-837-0027

Cover design by Sampathkumar J
Edited by Cathy Cruise
Interior design by Jetlaunch Layout Services

FIRST EDITION

This book is dedicated to all those who have worked side by side with us over the past twenty years, effectively putting the principles written about in these pages into practice. Together, we have accomplished much. We appreciate you.

Acknowledgments

It took a team to complete this book. We want to thank Austen and Judy, who helped make our writing better, as well as the Ignite Press team (Everett, Malia, and Zelda), who are the best publishers in the business.

A special thanks to our amazing Nikki, who was this book's project manager extraordinaire. *Mindset Matters* would not have happened without you, Nikki.

Table of Contents

Foreword by Daryle L. Doden

When I became the owner of Correct Craft in 2008—after several years as a minority owner and board member—the company was facing significant challenges. Then, things got worse. Just one month after I acquired 100 percent of the company, the Great Recession began.

Once the business was stabilized, I encouraged Bill to grow the Correct Craft platform and use it to honor God. I am proud that during my tenure as owner, the Correct Craft team has accomplished both goals.

Bill stepping down as Correct Craft's Chief Executive Officer represents a significant transition for the company and our team. However, after prayerful consideration, our Correct Craft board selected an outstanding successor in Zach Hutcheson. Zach will continue to drive growth while faithfully carrying forward Correct Craft's culture. The company's best days are still ahead.

The mindsets Bill and Zach have worked to memorialize in this book are deeply important. They have shaped the Correct Craft team's thinking for nearly two decades and have fueled extraordinary growth and impact. Together, these mindsets create an ownership mentality—one that consistently drives results.

I hope leaders take the time to thoughtfully engage with what Bill and Zach share on these pages. I am confident this book can make any leader or organization better.

Introduction

Correct Craft's growth over the past fifteen years has been nothing short of extraordinary, more than 25X. In 2009, our annual revenue was just over $39 million. By 2023, we hit our goal of becoming a billion-dollar company.

People often ask the secret behind this growth. After acknowledging the Correct Craft team, our standard response is simple: "Great culture and great strategic planning." But, while there may be a strategic planning book in our future, this book will focus on mindset, which is an important part of culture.

In two of Bill's previous books, *Making Life Better: The Correct Craft Story* and *Education of a CEO: Lessons for Leaders*, he explored Correct Craft's Culture Pyramid in depth.

We cannot overstate the impact of this culture pyramid; it is our North Star. It guides everything we do, from how we lead to how we serve our customers and communities. Our purpose is clear: to build boats to the Glory of God and to make life better for everyone who interacts with Correct Craft in any way.

This focus on culture has driven strong performance, which allows us to invest deeply in our people, our communities, and our businesses. Simply put, we would not be who we are today without our Culture Pyramid.

But There is More

Over the years, our team has developed a set of powerful mindsets that shape how we think, decide, and act. These mindsets quietly but consistently drive our success. In this book, we want to share them with you.

What Sparked our Focus on Mindset

Years ago, living in a college dorm at Florida Atlantic University (FAU), Bill went through a phase of reading self-improvement books. He didn't just find them interesting; he also believed they would help him prepare for a successful business career. Books like Dale Carnegie's *How to Win Friends and Influence People* and Maxwell Maltz's *Psycho-Cybernetics* were formative. They introduced Bill to a powerful idea: the way we think profoundly influences how successful we become.

After college, Bill began his career as a Certified Public Accountant (CPA) at the world's largest accounting firm. In that role, he audited and consulted with a wide range of businesses, each experiencing differing degrees of success. Later, while traveling around the globe as a speaker, Bill met with numerous leaders who shared both their successes and challenges. Serving on the boards of many for-profit and non-profit organizations provided yet another vantage point into how leaders think and operate.

Eventually, as the CEO of Correct Craft, a fast-growing company experiencing rapid growth and deeply engaged in mergers and acquisitions, Bill, joined by Zach and others on our team, regularly met with leaders from many organizations and reviewed their financial results. All this experience has allowed us to closely observe different leadership styles in action and to learn what works.

This broad perspective, involving numerous organizations and leaders, added to our experience with both acquisitions and running the forty-eight entities within our Correct Craft portfolio, has allowed us to test the correlation between mindset and success, and our findings have been fascinating.

Looking back, one lesson stands out above the rest: highly intelligent people often limit themselves because of how they think, while others who may be less gifted intellectually achieve extraordinary results because of how they think. As lifelong learners, we find this insight appealing.

Learnings Validated

What we have learned over the years about how our thought patterns are the primary determinant of our success or failure has been validated time and again. While it is important to be smart and work hard, much of what we achieve is a direct result of how we think—our mindset.

Emotion Trumps Logic

Unfortunately, very few people understand the effect of mindset. They are blinded by their own thinking, often called self-deception. Leaders believe their decisions are logic-based when most of the time they decide based on emotion.

Thinking that our decisions are logic-based is not surprising. For hundreds of years, economists and social scientists have believed people made decisions both logically and in their best interests. Some economists and social scientists still think that. However, modern research has clearly demonstrated that logic-based decision-making is a fallacy. Emotion trumps logic almost every time.

Our emotion-driven decision-making bias was identified in the groundbreaking, Nobel Prize-winning work of Daniel Kahneman and Amos Tversky. These Israeli psychologists proved that most of our decision-making is illogical. Together, they founded the science of behavioral economics, which is now widely studied and accepted. We have read many books on behavioral economics, and Bill spent a week studying the topic at Harvard Business School; the concept is powerful and corroborates the power of what we share in this book.

A strong mindset is powerful, involves thinking differently from the majority - and benefiting from a better paradigm. People who use the mindsets described in this book will have a huge advantage in almost every area of life. We have seen how powerful they are and want to share them to help others, including you.

We are not psychologists. But we are keen observers of people and the way their thinking drives success. Based on our decades of observation and experience, we are certain that the mindsets shared in the following pages will change your life for the better.

Culture Camp

About six times a year, we fly Correct Craft employees from around the country to Orlando for an experience we call "Culture Camp." During Culture Camp, our team discusses not only our Culture Pyramid in detail but also the mindsets shared in this book. We invest heavily in helping our team understand and live these principles because we know one thing to be true:

Mindset Matters!

A CEO Transition

Now, decades after reading those early books in his FAU dorm room and enjoying an insider view of countless organizations and their leaders, Bill is preparing to step down as Correct Craft CEO and hand the reins to Zach. During this time of CEO transition, we want to memorialize the mindsets that have helped drive Correct Craft's success for two decades so that our company's next generation of leaders will benefit from them. But this is not just for the Correct Craft team; any leader can benefit from these concepts.

That's Why We Wrote This Book

Just imagine… What would happen if you could think a little differently and enjoy much better results in every area of your life?

Keep reading; you're about to find out how.

Choose Impact

Many people have seen the familiar poster: a stunning seaside house, complete with a five-car garage filled with exotic sports cars. In big letters, the poster reads "JUSTIFICATION FOR HIGHER EDUCATION." Unfortunately, that poster has likely sent many people down a dangerous path.

Not that higher education is bad—it's great. We don't know anyone who encourages it more than we do, but that poster fosters a destructive mindset. It insinuates that happiness comes from having stuff. However, we have known many wealthy people, a lot of whom are very unhappy. Their money or other assets do not make them sad; their mindset does. The most effective and happy people chase impact, not rewards.

Chasing Impact: A Message to New MBA's and Lawyers

In 2023, Bill was honored to speak at Nova Southeastern University (NSU)'s commencement ceremony that celebrated the school's new master's in business administration (MBA) and law school graduates.

There were over 10,000 graduates, family, and friends during his commencement address. Bill shared a story illustrating the importance of pursuing impact with the graduates, their friends, and their families. Below is an excerpt from Bill's book *Faith Leap* that discusses that commencement address.

The idea I shared at that commencement ceremony was that we can have much more satisfying careers if we don't spend them chasing rewards but instead chase impact. This was probably hard for many of the graduates to comprehend, because a good portion of them had been studying for years to get the rewards that come with a successful career. However, as I shared with them during the ceremony, focusing primarily on rewards can be a trap. To make my point, I shared the story of two characters.

The first character, Adam, was an intelligent guy who did well in school and craved rewards. He wanted a nice house, a fancy and fast car, and luxurious vacations. These things are fine, but Adam had a mindset problem. Because he was so intent on chasing rewards, Adam jumped on what psychologists call the hedonic treadmill. The hedonic treadmill is a psychological term for the trap people chasing rewards fall into. In short, the hedonic treadmill gives the person on it occasional tastes of rewards to keep them running, but Adam and others on it don't notice the treadmill's ever-increasing speed and steeper incline. Every taste of a reward keeps those on the hedonic treadmill running faster, in search of more rewards while never being ultimately satisfied. Adam ended his career of chasing rewards exhausted, disappointed, and with broken relationships. The path he thought would provide rewards did give some, but they were unsatisfying. Adam ended up wondering why he'd wasted his career and life.

The other character I spoke about in my commencement speech was Oscar, a guy who decided to chase impact, not reward. Oscar was focused on making his organization, his team, and his community better. Sure, he liked nice things, but chasing them was not Oscar's primary mindset; he was focused on using his platform for good.

We can have much more satisfying careers if we don't spend them chasing rewards but instead chase impact. Oscar received a tremendous amount of satisfaction from his career because he was focused on helping people—what we at Correct Craft call "Making Life Better." This is the crazy part: Oscar's focus on impact made him a very valuable employee. Oscar was rewarded nicely, because every organization wants impact-oriented people on their team, and management will do all they can to recruit, retain, and reward them.

So Adam chased the rewards—looking out for number one—yet, despite occasional happiness, ended up miserable, unsatisfied, and exhausted. Oscar chased impact and ended up not only being satisfied but also getting the rewards Adam was chasing. By chasing impact, Oscar got the dual wins of both satisfaction and rewards.

The point I was sharing with the graduates was not a common one, but I knew if they listened and applied what I was sharing, it would change their lives dramatically for the better. Many studies have taught us that we don't find happiness by chasing either happiness or things we believe will bring pleasure. We find happiness by having a higher purpose and serving others. (For those interested, that graduation speech can be found on YouTube and is about 10 minutes long.)

After years of studying with a reward mindset, I am certain that some, maybe many, of the graduates listening to me that day found my words odd. Though clearly intelligent people, many of the graduates may have dismissed what I was saying, being focused instead on walking the stage, getting their diplomas, and chasing rewards.

Encouraging people to give up chasing rewards to instead chase impact may sound counterintuitive to those who have spent years studying to get a rewarding job.

Bill was making three points with the graduates. First, "stuff" does not bring happiness; it often brings the opposite. Second, happiness comes from chasing impact, not rewards. Third, chasing impact often leads to rewards because impact-driven people are valuable. So, chasing impact is the key to obtaining both happiness and rewards.

What Does it Mean to Chase Impact?

Decades of research studies have examined what makes people happy, and the results are so consistent that we are not sure why researchers keep investigating it. And, the findings are not only clear but also contrary to what most people think would make them happy. Happiness comes from a willingness to serve and help others, often helping those who can never repay what was done for them. Happiness comes from a selfless approach to life that tries to make everything and everyone around us better.

Chasing impact is just that: working to make the world around us better. This can be our local community, our family, those around the globe, and work team. When we are committed to an important purpose beyond ourselves, we are chasing impact.

Chasing Impact as a Team

The story of Bill joining Correct Craft is well-documented, and we won't repeat it all here. However, in summary, the company was a mess. Bill was the fifth CEO in five years; as if that did not signify enough of a challenge, the family that owned the company—while good people—could agree on little.

Correct Craft needed many changes, which eventually were implemented, but the biggest problem when Bill arrived was the company's poor culture. Bill told the team that we wanted to use our platform for good, but the employees didn't know whether they could trust him as the fifth CEO in as many years. Employees had heard promises before. Many doubted Bill would stay long enough to make a difference.

To jumpstart a culture reset, Bill made an unconventional decision: he took twenty-five employee volunteers to Tecate, Mexico, to build a house for a homeless family. Almost everyone thought it was a terrible idea. "We have a business crisis," they argued. "Why are we building a house in Mexico?" But the trip changed everything.

Bill writes about the story of this trip in a couple of his past books but below is an excerpt from *Faith Leap* with part of the story.

> *In hindsight, the impact of culture on Correct Craft's growth is clear; however, in early 2007, my thinking wasn't so clear. At the time, one thing was obvious: The organization needed a jolt to catalyze the start of our culture journey. So, despite some naysayers who thought a service trip was not where we should focus our time and energy, about 25 of us traveled to Tecate, Mexico.*
>
> *Our team worked very hard during the days we were in Tecate, living in the desert where the daily temperature was 110 degrees. We took showers by pouring lake water on our heads, soaping up, and rinsing off with more lake water. In* Education of a Traveler, *I write about this trip in detail, but suffice it to say here that the conditions were tough. Think sleeping in the desert, brutal heat, and bathing in lake water, kind of tough. However, before we left Tecate, our team of 25*

had built a small house and was honored to hand the keys to a previously homeless family of five in a very emotional ceremony.

After giving the keys to the new homeowners, our team headed to San Diego to catch our flight home. In a group meeting before the flight, I asked everyone to share their thoughts on the trip. It had been a very difficult few days, so I was unsure what they would say. Now I wish we had recorded that meeting, because it was one of the most powerful moments of my life. People said things like "best few days of my life," "I have never done anything so meaningful," and "I cannot wait to serve like this again."

Looking back with clear hindsight, I believe that trip was the turning point for our company. We were able to help a homeless family in Tecate, and those of us who went were also affected in a different but equally important way. Even those on our team who did not travel to Mexico with us saw that we had been able to help people who needed us, who would never be able to pay us back. Our team now had something bigger than just boats to build and our organizational mess to clean up. We were determined to use our platform for good, and it pointed Correct Craft in a great new direction.

Since that trip, I have traveled with our team to serve in Cambodia, India, Ethiopia, Uganda, Kenya, multiple Caribbean islands, and most of the Central American countries. The reaction of those who go on these service trips is always very similar to those on that first trip to Tecate. Even employees who choose not to join us on these trips are proud to work for a company of people who feel compassion for others and work to put action behind their feelings.

In this case, Bill's instincts were right, and that Mexico trip was a turning point for our company. It served as the spark that propelled us from a $39 million company in 2009 to a more than $1 billion company in 2023. It deeply affected those who went to Mexico, but it also had a significant impact on those employees who didn't go. Everyone realized that the talk about using our platform for good was not just empty words; we were doing it. We still had a lot of problems to fix in the business, but after that trip, most of us began to realize what we could do together once we got our mess cleaned up.

We were chasing impact.

People want to be part of something bigger than themselves, so chasing impact is not just a personal mindset but also an essential organizational mindset. People want to be inspired, not managed.

Many Self-Help Books are Wrong

There are a zillion self-help books available to those who want to get better or be happier, and over the past four decades, we have read several of them. The major problem with these books is that many of them give bad advice. They are heavily focused on being selfish—looking out for #1—and that leads to a life spent on the hedonic treadmill, and often, unhappiness rather than happiness.

In other words, it is hard to be happy if your own happiness is your primary motivation. People become happy by creating lives that affect others positively. John Bunyan, author of *Pilgrim's Progress*, said, "You have not lived today unless you have done something for someone who cannot repay you."

During our research for this book, we read an article from *Psychology Today* magazine. The article states, "Lasting happiness occurs when we invest in meaningful goals, relationships, and values..." Interestingly, it didn't mention the seaside house with a five-car garage full of exotic sports cars or any awards, recognition, or affirmation that so many people chase as rewards. It confirms the fact that happiness comes from being unselfish.

Why Choosing Impact is So Hard

As executives of a global company, we understand and appreciate the power of marketing. Marketers have done a great job encouraging us all to believe happiness is connected to whatever they are selling. Marketers never want you to be content; their job is to make people believe that happiness is contingent on buying their product.

When he was the world's richest person, John Paul Getty was asked how much was enough, and he reportedly, and famously, answered, "Just a little bit more." Getty's words help us understand exactly why the hedonic treadmill is so destructive. You cannot get to the end of it or win on it.

Everyone wants to be happy. Since we are conditioned to connect stuff with happiness, we are easily seduced by the "looking out for #1" ideology. We can fall into the trap of thinking, "I won't be happy without the stuff", and "the only way I am going to get this stuff is by looking out for myself." Unfortunately for the millions trapped in this thinking, it is a lie.

This is why choosing impact is not always the obvious choice; we have been programmed to think otherwise. But it is the right choice.

The Good, Even Great, News

The interesting—although counterintuitive—thing about chasing impact is that, while you are not prioritizing rewards, doing so often still delivers the rewards sought by those on the hedonic treadmill. And even better, it delivers those rewards without the negative effect of that treadmill.

Impact-focused people reap these rewards because they are highly valued. Few people want to deal with someone selfish, but an unselfish person is in demand and valuable.

However, you cannot fake it.

Bill took a weeklong course at the London School of Economics (LSE) called "Profit and Purpose." As part of the course, they discussed findings that indicate purpose-driven organizations perform better than those that focus solely on profit. The lessons from LSE validated what we learned at Correct Craft after the first Mexico trip, which we wrote about above. However, organizations that try to act purpose-driven just for financial benefits have worse results than they would if they weren't trying at all. People see through inauthenticity and manipulation, and those perceptions hurt the organization.

This lesson applies to individuals, too. If someone is chasing impact just because they believe rewards are best achieved that way, it won't work. Authenticity matters.

So Why Doesn't Everyone Know This?

If chasing impact makes someone happier and they can still get the rewards, how is this news? If it were true, wouldn't everyone already know it? Great questions! We are happy you asked; there are two answers to those questions.

First, we all have a selfish nature that makes us easily buy into the messages from self-help books and marketing. Marketers present cool stuff with a message that things will make us happy, and then the self-help folks tell us to be self-focused to get the cool stuff. The folks promoting these messages are often well-intentioned, good people who are not intentionally trying to harm you. However, they do not fully appreciate the power and benefits of chasing impact.

Second, the message of chasing impact lacks the marketing muscle that chasing rewards has. Billions are spent promoting a message that we need to be self-focused to be happy. Unfortunately, that message is wrong.

We have seen the power of chasing impact firsthand.

Four Elephants in the Room

While finishing this chapter, we thought of some questions folks may have about chasing impact. So, we want to address them. The four elephants in the room are below.

1.   What about people who seem selfish and happy?

Some people are both selfish and happy, but there are fewer than you might think. If most research teaches us that happiness comes from being unselfish, we shouldn't assume that just because a selfish person projects happiness, it is a genuine emotion. Appearances can be deceiving.

Think about your social media accounts. Do they project the real person, or are they highlights for others to see? Sometimes, what we see of others is not the real them, just an image they want to project about themselves. Several years ago, a friend of Zach's posted on social media that she had the most wonderful husband ever and boldly proclaimed his greatness and her love for him. It was sweet but untrue. Six weeks later, she left him.

We have seen similar things many times. The only person who can honestly know their level of happiness or joy is ourselves.

2.   What about those who chase impact but don't get the rewards?

Some may think of people who have pursued impact their entire lives and never received the material rewards others chase. There are a couple of things to consider about this. First, not everyone who chases rewards gets them, but everyone who chases rewards experiences the stress of doing so. Second, people chasing impact may enjoy rewards like all of us, but it is not what drives them. They still get joy and happiness from chasing impact, even without the rewards.

Those considering this question may see chasing impact as a path to rewards, but don't think that way. It doesn't work, and others see through it.

3. Aren't you both executives who use marketing to sell boats to people all over the world?

Correct Craft sells boats in dozens of countries, and marketing plays a big part in our business strategy. Marketing is not bad. However, our mindset is broken when we get caught up in marketing and believe what is being promoted by a company is our key to happiness.

Specifically, regarding boats, we embrace "Blue Mind," an idea explored and written about by our late friend Wallace "J" Nichols in his book of the same name. We encourage anyone interested to pick up a copy of "J's" book. The essence of it is that we are healthier physically, emotionally, mentally, and spiritually when we are near, on, in, or under the water. We have seen this firsthand with our own families; being on the water helps build strong relationships that last for years.

There is nothing specifically wrong with boats or anything else that may be marketed to you. It is your mindset that matters.

4. What about you, Bill, and Zach? You both have had successful careers and have nice stuff. Now you tell us not to want that stuff?

Fair question. Remember, it is your mindset that matters, not having stuff.

We have both been very blessed and enjoyed successful careers. However, neither of us thinks you can find anyone who would say we are reward-driven, because we are not. We don't like holding ourselves out as an example for anything, but we—perhaps with an obvious bias—believe we have been impact-driven and want to use our platform for good.

Of course, we each have a family to support and want to be treated fairly. In short, we have focused on chasing impact, which has led us to getting rewards. We could be self-deceived—most of us are—but we want to make the world better and use our Correct Craft platform for good.

Final Thoughts

This chapter was tough to write because we are trying to convey a counterintuitive idea. Chasing impact brings significantly more happiness and joy and doesn't reduce your odds of getting the rewards. You're not giving anything up by chasing impact, but you are significantly increasing the probability of happiness and joy.

This isn't the last time we will consider a counterintuitive idea. Let's move on to Mindset #2.

Chapter 1 Summary

- We can chase rewards or impact.
- We are conditioned to believe happiness comes from rewards.
- Chasing rewards leads to life on the hedonic treadmill.
- The happiest and most effective people choose to pursue impact.
- The best life is unselfish and focused on making life better for others, including folks who can never pay them back.
- Chasing impact often leads to rewards without the hedonic treadmill.

Chapter 2

Be a Learner

As a confident thirteen-year-old boy, Bill spent an extraordinary amount of time thinking about driving (you probably assumed we were going to say girls, which would have been equally correct). The idea of the independence that driving would provide Bill was intoxicating: taking himself to school, going out on a date, and having the freedom to go wherever he wanted were all very appealing. It seemed ludicrous that the state of Florida would deny a driver's license to someone who felt so ready to take the wheel.

Bill was mentally prepared for the road and was certain his driving would be exemplary.

Until he proved otherwise.

An Accident and a Lesson

Bill learned how bad his thirteen-year-old driving was one morning in the school parking lot. He saw a friend—we will call her Cindy, because that was her name—who had just turned sixteen. Cindy was driving a brand-new car she had been given for her birthday. That morning's trip to school was her first solo journey in the new car, and the odometer hadn't even reached twenty-five miles.

When Bill saw Cindy and her new car, he was happy for her, but also envious, anticipating one day driving himself to school. That's when he had a not-so-great idea. He asked Cindy if he could drive her car, and after he laid on some charm, she agreed, unfortunately. You probably already know where this is going. Bill climbed into the driver's seat, put the car in reverse, and, with absolutely no sense or idea of how to drive, backed the car into a passing school bus.

The result: Cindy's brand-new vehicle, driven less than twenty-five miles, was wrecked by a thirteen-year-old boy who had no clue what he was doing but thought he did. Thankfully, no one was hurt. Cindy, if you are reading this, Bill is still VERY, VERY sorry.

If you are wondering, there were consequences. Bill spent two holiday seasons selling Christmas cards to reimburse his parents for the cost of the damage. There was also a potent lesson in the accident; it was a great example of how we can all suffer from being a **knower**. Bill was completely certain of his ability to drive despite a lack of experience, and it is still a powerful reminder now, decades later. As Bill proved by wrecking Cindy's new car, a knower can feel 100% right and actually be 100% wrong.

A Lesson from Harvard

No one is exempt from the seduction of being a knower. In *Education of a CEO,* Bill wrote about taking classes at Harvard Business School. At Harvard, Bill observed very smart people stick to their position regarding a case study even though the professor had conclusively proven their positions were wrong. They were knowers. Although some readers have already read *Education of a CEO*, the Harvard story is still worth repeating below.

> *During my fourth course at Harvard Business School, it was interesting to hear the professor begin the class with the Carter Racing case study. Unfortunately, I couldn't participate in the case study because this was my third time hearing it presented, and I knew about the surprise ending. However, knowing how the case was going to culminate gave me an interesting perspective as I watched my classmates wrestle with it.*
>
> *My fellow students grappling with the case study were no slouches. They were ninety executives from all over the globe, many of them CEOs. However,*

despite their pedigrees, the case study progressed and concluded, predictably, exactly as it does when presented dozens of times each year at universities around the world.

In the Carter Racing case, students are required to make a decision between "Go" and "No Go" alternatives, and a high percentage of them initially choose to "Go." After the students have presented their decisions, the professor slowly releases more and more information that clearly demonstrates the correct decision is "No Go." On top of the analytical information that clearly demonstrates that "No Go" is the correct decision, the professor releases additional information that creates a strong emotional argument for the "No Go" decision.

Finally, the professor concludes the case by presenting a linear regression analysis that demonstrates a ninety-nine percent probability that the "Go" decision is bad. At that point, the decision is simple, right? Not so much.

Each time I have seen the Carter Racing case presented, about ten to fifteen percent of the esteemed class continue to stick with their "Go" decision, even after hearing overwhelming evidence that it is a bad choice. It sounds crazy, but we, too, are all subject to those same blind spots. Most people prefer being a "knower" over a "learner." We all get trapped by our own perspective, but to reach your full potential as a leader, you must seek truth; you must be a learner.

We Limit Ourselves

We are all limited by our own experience and easily self-deceived. Ninety percent of people believe they are in the top 50% of drivers, and it is pretty clear that this is not possible. Leaders will limit themselves until they become humble enough to realize there is a LOT we don't know. We sometimes illustrate this when speaking at events by putting a small dot on a large whiteboard. We explain that the whiteboard represents all there is to know, and the small dot shows what we each actually know.

Knower vs. Learner

The opposite of being a knower is being a **_learner_**. We become learners when we view every situation not as an opportunity to prove ourselves right but as an opportunity to grow or learn.

Generally, knowers seek validation, while learners seek the truth. Validation feels good, which is enticing, while truth can sometimes make us uncomfortable. However, who wants to go through a lifetime of false thinking? A lifetime of feeling good for believing things that are not true? That is self-deception, and it is the number one thing that keeps people from reaching their potential.

That's right. The number one thing that holds people back from achieving success is not their company, boss, upbringing, spouse, or any other external circumstance; it is themselves, particularly their own thinking. We limit ourselves, which is why we have identified being a learner as so important; once we become learners, everything else becomes easier.

To be clear:

- **A learner** consumes information with a willingness—maybe even a hope—of seeing things in a new way or having their mind changed.
- **A knower** consumes information to validate what they already think or believe.

Are You a Learner or a Knower?

You may be reading this, thinking you are a learner, or at least thinking, "Gosh, I hope I am a learner." However, in our experience, most people are not learners; they are knowers. Below are some questions that will help you determine whether you are a knower or a learner.

Do you resist having your mind changed? Very few people seek the truth; instead, most people want validation. This pursuit of validation leads to a perspective known as confirmation bias. Confirmation bias can be seen in all areas of our lives as we look at any set of facts and see them through our own worldview to confirm what we already think. Again, knowers don't want their minds to change; they want validation.

Using ourselves as an example for anything is not fun because we know how short we fall in so many areas. However, over time, we have trained ourselves to enjoy having our minds changed. Strangely enough, having our minds changed is fun and gives us a bit of an endorphin rush. We know that it's weird. But, if you prefer feeling right to having your mind changed, you are probably a knower.

Do you get all your news from the same source? As a bit of a news junkie, Bill has seen firsthand how news, especially from television, has become less factual and mostly biased for commentary. While most of his news comes from various non-television sources, Bill tends to watch television news during significant events. Sometimes, changing between the top two or three news channels during those events gives different perspectives and is fascinating. It's like totally different events have occurred depending on the channel. Even worse, some news folks no longer view their job as reporting the news; they want to tell people how the news should be interpreted.

Of course, fewer of us get our news today from television. However, wherever you get yours—social media, an internet influencer, or some other source—there is almost always bias.

This bias in news reporting is a substantial barrier to critical thinking. Most people watch a specific news channel or influencer not for accurate news but for someone to make them feel good about how they already think. Learners want to gather information from several sources and then use their critical thinking skills to decide what to think.

If you almost always get your news from the same source, you are probably a knower.

Do you mostly read the same types of books? Both of us love reading; between audiobooks, e-readers, and actual old-fashioned bound books, we each consume dozens of books a year. Often, people will scratch their heads after hearing the title of a book one of us is reading and say something like, "I wouldn't expect you to be reading that."

We see little value in reading something that makes us feel good about what we already know or believe. We want to read material that will stretch or challenge our thinking and help us build empathy.

A few years ago, when the U.S.A. was struggling with racial tensions, Bill decided to learn as much as he could about the Black experience in our country. Bill read at least fifteen books—both nonfiction and fiction—written by Black authors to learn more about what it's like to live a life he had not experienced as a white man. The books were eye-opening and significantly broadened Bill's view. They also increased his empathy for those who have a very different experience in our country than he does.

If you usually read books that confirm what you already think, you are probably a knower.

Do the people you spend time with all think like you? This might be the most challenging test, because we all want to be with people like ourselves. We gravitate toward people who think like us. Whether it is religion, politics, sports teams, or any other affinity, we enjoy people like us. It's human nature.

Most folks avoid others who think differently from them because it is hard to discuss differences without emotion. Since emotion trumps logic, winning an emotional argument is almost impossible.

However, though having a non-emotional discussion with some-one who thinks differently requires discipline and self-control, it is energizing. It is also a huge opportunity to learn.

Bill has spent a lot of time in Washington, D.C. over the past fif-teen years and has met some great people. Early in his D.C. days, Bill became friends with an incredibly brilliant gentleman who was the CEO of a technology company in the Midwest. Bill respected this man and, one evening, enjoyed an after-dinner conversation with him about highly controversial and often emotional issues on which they held different views. They had unique perspectives, but they both respected and listened to each other. Bill was so excited by the con-versation that he couldn't sleep that night; he had learned a lot.

If you spend most of your time with people who think just like you do, you are likely a knower.

Do you spend a lot of energy justifying your decisions? We all want to make good decisions, and after we have made them, we want to believe we did the right thing. Some people will even seek out pos-itive reviews of something they've bought, even after the purchase, to confirm their decision.

Justifying our decisions is especially compelling when we explain our decision to others. If the decision worked out, it is because we are smart. If it didn't, well, that is because of unexpected circumstances or just bad luck.

If you spend a lot of energy justifying past decisions, especially those that didn't work out, you are likely a knower.

Do you quickly feel like an expert after learning something new? Another knowing trap, which even the best leaders can fall into, is the Dunning-Kruger effect. In its simplest terms, the Dunning-Kruger effect is when you know a little bit about something but think you fully understand it. This is particularly prevalent when someone learns something new and immediately is confident that they totally understand the subject well, despite knowing very little.

If you fall victim to feeling like an expert after learning just a little about something, you are likely a knower.

The above are a few ways to determine if you are a learner or a knower. If you answered yes to any of the above questions, there is a good chance that you are a knower.

So, how can we be learners?

We can either approach life as learners or suffer the consequences of being knowers. Those consequences are high. Knowers stay trapped in their own thinking, which makes them feel good but also results in living a lie. They not only fail to reach their potential but also go through life deceived. Who wants to live like that? The good news is this is a choice. The following are some ways to help anyone become a learner.

Acknowledge the reality of self-deception: The first step to changing your world in a big way is to acknowledge the problem of self-deception. This is really tough for most people because they feel so right about their thinking. For those who want to improve in this area, we recommend a number of books in the appendix.

Decide to seek truth rather than comfort: This, too, is hard because most people believe that what they already think is the truth, and it makes them feel good.

Surround yourself with people who will disagree with you: Make sure the folks around you understand that you want their opinions. And to prove that, do not criticize those opinions while brainstorming. Or, often, even harder, don't get emotional with someone for sharing their perspective.

Read material that broadens your perspective: We are not afraid of seeking truth, even if it conflicts with what we currently think. And that perspective has helped us materially over the years.

Travel to different places: Bill has had the opportunity to visit more than 110 countries, and each visit has expanded his paradigms. You don't need to visit 110 countries, or even travel far, but try to visit some places that are new to you; you will be surprised by how your view expands. Bill writes more about how this works in his book *Education of a Traveler*.

Watch different news sources: This point may be the toughest of all for some people. Neither of us are big TV viewers, but as we previously noted, we occasionally have tried to watch different news programs, especially after a big event. The days of news programs sharing actual news are long over. They have become big echo chambers, and people tend to listen to news channels that make them feel good about their views. Mix it up a little by watching something different.

Be contrarian: Someone once said, "Insanity in individuals is rare, but insanity in groups is very common." Bill experienced this personally several years ago in Reno, Nevada, with a bunch of guys who decided it would be fun to ride a mechanical bull. It was not his finest moment, but it was a good example of herd behavior that unfortunately left him with a leg injury. Many scientific studies have shown that most people are easily persuaded by what the crowd is thinking. This, combined with the common information effect, which states teams tend to focus mostly on the areas where they agree, can be dangerous for decision-makers. Our team at Correct Craft uses a tool called Thinking Hats, from the great book *Six Thinking Hats*, authored by Edward de Bono. This tool helps us see differing perspectives, including contrarian ones called "black hat."

Even the Catholic church has historically appointed a "devil's advocate" to look for reasons not to canonize someone being considered for sainthood. We need to consider contrarian views in our thinking and decision-making.

Don't let people "anchor" you: This happens when someone traps you into thinking a certain way. An example of this would be when a salesperson gets you thinking about a high price early, so any deal below that price seems reasonable. Also, the "decoy effect" leads us to get captured by something that is not significant to the decision being made. Be careful and aware; the best persuaders are adept at framing your perspective, which can lead to a suboptimal view of any situation.

For Clarity

A learner seeks truth and is open to expanding or changing their thinking. A knower wants to validate what they already think. Being a learner is a mindset shift that will dramatically improve your life.

A Couple of Final Thoughts

In her excellent book *Mindset* (discussed more in the next chapter), Carol Dweck shares research about the benefits of a growth mindset versus a fixed mindset. Folks with a growth mindset are learners, and Dweck's book is a mighty reinforcer of the importance of being one. Being a learner provides a robust return well beyond the specific items learned; it is a different way of thinking that creates a foundation for continuous improvement. As the learning increases, it becomes synergistic, which will dramatically improve your effectiveness in every area of life.

A final benefit of being a learner is that it will significantly increase your energy level. When you acknowledge you could be wrong, it is incredibly freeing, and energizing.

We have both worked with folks who put enormous pressure on themselves to be right all the time. It takes a lot of energy to believe you know everything about everything, and even more energy to make people think you know everything. Changing your self-identity from being a knower to being a learner will make life more exciting, and it will be liberating. You will enjoy new energy beyond what you could think possible. Just imagine.

The importance of being a learner is one of our core beliefs and values. Speaking to more than 10,000 people at a 2019 University of Central Florida graduation ceremony, Bill had only a few minutes to give a commencement address. Most of the folks there just wanted to graduate or see their loved one's graduate, but Bill was given time to share one lesson that some students might recall and, hopefully, even use to change their lives. It was his one brief chance to influence those graduates—and their friends and families—and Bill used that time to speak about the difference between being a learner and a knower. (For anyone interested, the speech is on YouTube.)

As we consider Mindsets that help us think about success, near the top of the list is being a learner. It is a foundational concept for our Correct Craft team. We will learn about several more concepts in the chapters ahead, including the next chapter, where we further discuss the importance of a growth mindset.

Chapter 2 Summary

- While most people are knowers, being a learner is a significant life hack.
- A learner seeks truth, not validation.
- The easiest way to know if we are knowers is whether we are looking for validation or feel like we need to be right.
- Be intentional about being learners.
- Enjoy having your mind changed.
- Embracing the idea of being a learner will significantly improve your effectiveness in every area of life.

Growth vs. Fixed Mindset

Zach believes the greatest gift his parents gave to him is the confidence that he can do anything he sets his mind to. While there are obvious limits to this, for example, his shaky hands make a career in medicine unrealistic, it's the mindset that matters. With persistent effort and hard work, nothing will stand in his way. That last part is important to understand; it's not natural talent that drives success. Instead a person with a growth mindset realizes it's the willingness to work hard to achieve a desired goal that drives success.

In her previously mentioned well-known book, *Mindset,* Carol Dweck explains how people think about their abilities and success profoundly shapes their performance, resilience, and growth. She distinguishes between people who have a "growth mindset" and those who have a "fixed mindset." For leaders to reach their potential and optimize their organization's results, they must have a growth mindset.

Mindset

People with a growth mindset believe that their abilities can be developed through learning, effort, and persistence. They see challenges as opportunities to learn and grow. In contrast, people with a fixed mindset believe that intelligence, talent, and abilities are innate and static. As discussed in Chapter 2, folks with a fixed mindset are almost always a "knower."

A knower believes you either have it, or you don't. They see challenges as a threat and work to avoid them to protect their image. Interestingly, most people have a fixed mindset, and they don't even realize it.

It is well known that both of us love to read

One of Zach's favorite parts of reading a new book is sharing it with friends. Many mornings on his drive into work, Zach will call Thomas, his good friend and coworker, to talk about what they are currently reading. They enjoy recommending new books to each other and sharing their thoughts on any new topic they read about. They can talk for hours discussing interesting points of a book, often uncovering insights the other person had not considered. Thomas's perspective is always thought-provoking, leading to a fun and spirited conversation. Thomas has a growth mindset, and their conversations make them both better.

Think Like a Winner

There are endless debates about who is the greatest basketball player of all time. Michael Jordan, Kobe Bryant, and LeBron James are the three players most often in the conversation. All three have led their teams to multiple NBA championships, individually won NBA MVP awards, and have played in many All-Star games. While fans may disagree who deserves the Greatest of all Times (GOAT) title, there is no argument that all three are very talented basketball players.

While Michael Jordan, Kobe Bryant, and LeBron James are all known for their NBA success, what's not always known is the work behind the talent. After being cut from his high school basketball team, Michael Jordan was at school every morning by 6 AM to practice. Kobe Bryant's former teammates tell stories of him getting to practice 2 hours early and shooting with the lights out. Even in his 23rd season as a professional basketball player, LeBron is known to outwork the rookies much younger than him.

These athletes have a growth mindset and think like a winner. They have the mental toughness, heart, and dedication to be the greatest ever. When times get difficult, they find the will to dig down deep and overcome.

Leaders with a growth mindset who think like a winner distinguish themselves from the rest. The most successful leaders are willing to look challenges in the face, including their own failures, while maintaining faith that they will overcome in the end.

Failure is Information

In 2018, Correct Craft launched Watershed Innovation, a company dedicated to explore, research, and apply disruptive innovations to our businesses. Watershed Innovation was a direct result of our team's growth mindset.

The Watershed Innovation team looks at potential disruptive innovations that could someday put one of our current Correct Craft companies out of business. We know that innovation is happening, computational power is increasing, and if we are not intentional about innovating, Correct Craft will be left in the past.

One of the recent projects at Watershed Innovation has been to integrate advanced robotics into Correct Craft's boat manufacturing plants. With the recent advancements in artificial intelligence, implementing robotics into a low-volume and high-variation production process suddenly became a reality. A team from across Correct Craft was formed to kick off the project and learn everything they could about these latest robot technologies, and eventually, a recommendation was made to invest in an Autonomous Mobile Robot (AMR) solution at Nautique. This solution was designed to carry upholstered parts from station to station as they were being built, and eventually directly to the manufacturing line to be installed into the boat waiting for it. This would be a huge improvement to the process, while also being a low-risk robot deployment before tackling more substantive projects.

Unfortunately, as the project progressed, several unforeseen software challenges developed. The team worked closely with the vendor to try to resolve them, but ultimately made the decision to cancel the project. While the team was clearly disappointed in the results, they had a growth mindset and viewed this failure as a great learning experience. Through this failure, they gained a significant amount of experience in advanced robotics and were able to apply these learnings to future projects. Shortly after, because of a growth mindset, the Watershed Innovation and Nautique teams were able to learn from their failures to implement a robot in their assembly line to help safely install heavy windshields onto the boats. The growth mindset to use failure as an opportunity to learn gave the team a big leap forward in their robotics initiative.

Too Great to Fail

Tim Irwin's book *Derailed* reviews the careers of six successful business leaders who lost their way. They all seemed to demonstrate the traits of great leaders, but each destroyed their careers, and sometimes the businesses they ran, through a failure of humility, self-control, and courage.

Leaders with a fixed mindset believe that they are naturals at business, and don't invest in areas like learning, recruiting and retaining talent, and innovation. The failure to invest in these areas will cause great leaders and great companies to lose their way. The leaders and companies that do invest in those things are the ones that leap to greatness and stay there. They have a growth mindset.

Abundance

Zach has a busy family. His two sons, George and Parker, are active in sports and their church, and his wife Christine gracefully keeps track of it all.

Not long ago, after Zach got home from work, and Christine got the boys home from flag football practice and piano lessons, George and Parker decided they wanted tacos for dinner. Being a busy day, neither Zach nor Christine had time to prepare anything for dinner. Luckily, technology was able to solve their problem. Christine pulled out her phone to order tacos from a local favorite restaurant, and within 30 minutes, their dinner was at the door.

George and Parker have an amazing mindset advantage in life. Growing up in an era of technology, they are used to being able to solve problems of convenience with their phones (or their parents' phones for now). Because of their growth mindset, and their early experiences, they naturally think with abundance.

When leaders think with abundance they have the belief that there are enough resources and opportunities to go around, and that growth is possible through learning, collaboration, and effort. People who think with abundance focus on expanding the pie instead of taking a bigger piece of the pie that exists today. They think "If I help others succeed, we all get better" instead of "If someone else wins, I lose."

What Mindset Am I In?

One of Dweck's most important insights is that people do not operate exclusively from one mindset. Most people shift between growth and fixed mindsets depending on the situation. Stress, ego, and high stakes can pull anyone toward a fixed mindset.

You can identify which mindset you are operating from by paying attention to how you think, feel, and act when things get difficult, especially under pressure. Dweck suggests assessing how you respond to the following:

Your reaction to a challenge

A fixed mindset avoids situations where struggle is likely.
A growth mindset embraces challenges, even when success is uncertain.
Ask yourself: Do I choose the safe path, or the path that will stretch me?

Your response to failure

A fixed mindset finds failure discouraging.
A growth mindset sees failure as a learning opportunity.
Ask yourself: Am I worried about how failure makes me look, or what it can teach me?

How you view effort

A fixed mindset believes effort means a lack of natural ability.
A growth mindset sees effort as the path to mastery.
Ask yourself: Do I admire what looks easy, or what has been earned?

How you handle feedback

A fixed mindset becomes defensive and discounts feedback.
A growth mindset values feedback and reflects on how to apply it.
Ask yourself: Am I protecting my image, or pursuing improvement?

This simple self-assessment can help you recognize your current mindset. Since mindset is a choice, choosing a growth mindset dramatically improves the odds of long-term success.

Final Thoughts

Having a growth mindset is contagious to those around you. We encourage you to step outside your comfort zone and embrace challenges as opportunities to learn. Failure is not the verdict on your abilities; it is the path to success.

In the next chapter, we will discuss why focusing on results is an important part of having a growth mindset.

Chapter 3 Summary

- A growth mindset is the path to mastery. High performers don't avoid hard things—they lean into them.
- People with a growth mindset believe that their abilities can be developed through learning, effort, and persistence.
- People with a fixed mindset believe that intelligence, talent, and abilities are innate and static.
- People with a growth mindset see failure as information, not as final.
- It's nearly impossible to maintain success with a fixed mindset.
- People don't have one mindset; they have both. Ask yourself which mindset you have as you approach a challenge.
- A growth mindset is contagious.

Chapter 4

Results > Activity

Our Correct Craft team has completed numerous acquisitions over the past fifteen years. Every deal is different, but there is one part of the acquisition process that is almost always the same. At some point before we acquire a new company, our team will meet with the executives of the company being acquired to get to know them and assess how we would all work together. The comments of the people we are interviewing are very predictable. They want us to know how busy they are.

Why? Because busyness has become a proxy for importance which causes leaders to equate activity with value.

This misattribution of value happens because many people's self-identity is based on their own perception that they are busy. So, they believe other folks will value them for being busy, too. This is a critical mindset and leadership mistake.

It Seems Obvious, But it's Not

A key mindset leaders need to embrace is that results are always more important than activity. We know, it seems simple and obvious as you read that, but it is not in real life. Leaders get so much intrinsic value from feeling busy that they miss the importance and value of focusing on results over activity.

A leader who changes their mindset to focus on results over activity will be shocked at how much their performance improves and how much more time they gain. Being focused on results creates laser-like attention on what needs to be done and how to accomplish it. This mindset shift alone can change your life.

Parkinson's Law

So why does everyone feel busy, regardless of their results? Parkinson's Law helps us understand this. Basically, Parkinson's Law states that most people pace their work to fit the time allotted. In other words, we will get the required work done in the time we are given to do it. And because many leaders' self-identity requires them to feel busy, they fill up their time and believe they are busy, not realizing they could accomplish so much more.

Some real-life examples of this are:

- Schedule a one-hour meeting, and the entire hour will be used. Often, the same topic could have been covered—many times better and certainly more efficiently—in thirty minutes.
- If a report is due in two weeks, it will take two weeks to complete. With a two-day deadline, the quicker report will likely reach the same conclusions.
- Allocate an afternoon to clean out your email inbox, and it will take that long. Limit yourself to an hour, and it will still get done.

So, when Parkinson's Law combines with a desire for the importance that feeling busy gives folks, the result is predictable: leaders will confuse value with being busy more than getting results, even if they don't overtly realize it. Honestly, we believe most leaders have this problem. They unknowingly prize activity over results, and both they and their organizations pay the price.

Swirling: Activity Without Progress

Does your organization have problems that never seem to get resolved? Is your team better at identifying challenges than overcoming them? Does your team talk about a problem repeatedly without fixing it? If so, bells and sirens should be going off because your organization is at significant risk. You are experiencing what we at our company call "*swirling*."

Swirling happens because it is far easier to identify problems than achieve the results needed to solve them. It is also easier to throw out potential solutions when you are not responsible for the results or unintended consequences. It is much tougher to develop and implement a solution under the full weight of responsibility for the decision's impact, including unintended consequences; a situation that causes even smart leaders consternation.

Decision-making is hard. Most meaningful decisions involve probability, not certainty. If the decision were obvious or easy, it's likely someone else would have already made it. Even when the decision has a 90% probability of being right, it will still be wrong one out of the ten times you make it. If either fear of failure or being wrong causes a leader to need a 100% certain decision, swirling is the result.

Swirling is dangerous. It bogs down an organization when it needs to be nimble to reach its potential to achieve its needed results. Swirling is also de-energizing to teams that experience it. If your organization tends to swirl, we guarantee you have the potential to improve your results.

Years ago, Zach worked with a gentleman who had an excruciatingly difficult time making decisions. His inbox was known as the "black hole." He hated deciding, and if prompted, would delay by saying he needed even more information. This was incredibly demotivating to his team; while he struggled to decide, he was an expert at swirling. This struggle caused Zach's colleague to fall short of obtaining the results his team needed.

Avoiding Swirling

Fortunately, while it is easy to fall into swirling, the best leaders make sure it does not happen at their organizations. Below are several ways to stop it:

- Create clarity. As with fixing many organizational issues, creating clarity is the first thing you can do to avoid swirling. Our team does this by asking, "What is the problem we are trying to solve?" It is amazing how that brief question can cause a team to refocus and create clarity around the issue at hand.

- Beware of diminishing returns. Like many other leaders, we want to do things right. However, sometimes the effort to get from 97% right to 100% right isn't worth the time. Or as one friend of ours will say, "The remaining juice isn't worth the squeeze." Often, the amount of time that it takes to get from 97% to 100% keeps leaders from getting several other goals accomplished. Chasing diminishing returns can be costly to overall results.

- Seek different perspectives. Often, swirling happens when the team gets hijacked by one perspective, usually negative, and cannot find a way to get past it. Getting out of this situation requires forcing yourself to expand your perspective and see the situation from a different point of view, which will frequently break the logjam. The previously mentioned book *Six Thinking Hats*, written by Edward de Bono, has been hugely helpful in assisting us and our team see any situation from different perspectives; every leader should read it.

- Have a trigger word. When our team is swirling, someone will announce we are "swirling." Having a trigger word that forces everyone to realize you're swirling is very helpful.

- Don't use the "I need more information" excuse. Certainly, leaders need adequate and accurate information to make good decisions. However, continually asking for more information is a deflection used by leaders who are struggling to decide. Doing so does not fool anyone; your team knows what you are doing.

- Decide. If collaboration among the team does not result in a decision, then the leader needs to make it. In an ideal world, when an organization is trying to find the solution to a challenge, there is collaboration that includes a robust debate but ends with an obvious decision. Of course, that's an ideal world, but it doesn't always happen like that for us in the real world. A leader must be prepared to decide; mulling it over endlessly is frustrating to the team and results in the diminishing returns noted above.

- The group must commit. When the debate is over and the team has either come to a collaborative decision or a leader has decided the path forward, it is time to commit and execute. Even worse than pre-decision swirling is post-decision swirling. To use a football analogy, once the quarterback makes a call, everyone better be running the same play.

Leaders who want to focus on results must make sure they are not swirling.

More on Creating Clarity

It is impossible for your team to focus on results if they don't have clarity regarding their leader's expectations. For example, we believe that the CEO of Correct Craft must provide clarity on the following things:

- Our Mission – Building Boats to the Glory of God
- Our Why – Making Life Better
- Our Vision – Currently $2 billion in annual sales by 2030, all employees understand and embrace our culture, lead the industry in monetizing global trends, and be nationally recognized as a company that impacts everyone's lives for the better
- Our Values – Reflected in our Culture Pyramid
- Our Strategic Plans – These are different for each Correct Craft company
- Our Annual Plans – Basically, each Correct Craft company's yearly budget

In short, if a leader supplies clarity regarding the expectations in each of these areas and hires the right people, the results will come.

Most Leaders Report Results. The Best Leaders Drive Them

Leaders like to take credit when results are good; it is a natural response. However, when results aren't good, the same leaders are quick to provide external factors to explain subpar outcomes. How can great outcomes always be a result of the leader's exceptional leadership ability, while disappointing outcomes are always a result of external factors beyond their control? The sad reality is that many leaders don't drive results; they just report them, taking credit where they can while blaming outside factors when things go awry.

For example, during the COVID economic boom, leaders in many markets enjoyed sharing how well they were doing. When asked if they were benefiting from tailwinds provided by either the pandemic or the massive government deficit spending during that time, they downplayed anything that might have helped get the positive results. Instead, they credited both their leadership and preparation.

But what happens when the results aren't so good? Suddenly, the sub-par results are not because of their leadership but because they are victims of bad circumstances.

Bad circumstances, including negative market changes, do occur and are often not the leader's fault. However, the best leaders will ensure their organization performs well in any environment; that's driving results. Their organization's results may be affected by market changes, but the best leaders optimize their results in any market. And they never lose money.

We have worked with leaders who try to distance themselves from a situation when failure seems possible. However, results-driven leaders step in and do whatever is necessary to ensure failure does not occur. Poor leaders try to distance themselves from difficult situations, but the best leaders take ownership and move toward challenges; they will not let their teams fail.

No good leader wants to just go along for the ride, either taking credit for good results or deflecting blame when results are below expectations. They want to have an impact and be responsible for their organization's results.

Be Proactive

Leaders who drive results are proactive, not reactive. They think strategically, which requires looking ahead to identify market changes before they happen and then preparing their organization for those upcoming changes. They see challenges as opportunities and plan to turn them into great results.

Take Ownership

Leaders who drive results also take ownership of either good or bad results. This may be the most critical determinant of a great leader. Someone who accepts ownership of any situation and is determined that the results will be good, regardless of the circumstances, is likely a great leader. Often, we tell leaders that when their team members feel circumstances are hopeless, those leaders must take ownership of the situation, put it on their own backs, and make positive things happen. It can be scary to step up and take ownership, but we know no faster way to learn, grow, and prepare for an even more significant role.

Driving Results at Correct Craft

How a leader drives results depends on their role and range of responsibility, which can vary for different leaders. Each leader's role is different, but the CEO of Correct Craft can drive results as follows:

- Provide clarity, which we discussed above.
- Ensure we have the right "Who's" – As discussed in the next chapter, when we have a challenge at Correct Craft, the view of our team is almost always "Who, not How." At our company,

as with any organization, results always begin with having the right team in place, and we understand the importance of having the right people in the right roles. It is the best way we can drive results at our company–ensure we have the right people on our team, and be willing to make a necessary ending when needed. Without the right people, nothing else matters. We will elaborate on this in a later chapter.

- Invest in leaders – Capital allocation is one of a CEO's most important responsibilities. And there is no investment with a higher return than investing in your team. Sometimes, other leaders may not see this because they consider employee development as an expense instead of an investment with a high return. Or they are afraid that they will make employees more valuable, which will help them find other jobs. However, as the late Zig Ziglar used to say, "It is better to invest in your people and have them leave than not invest in your people and have them stay." Leaders who drive results are always looking for ways to develop their people.

- Provide energy – Leaders must provide their team with energy to get results. We emphasize five things leaders must do to provide this energy: Create clarity, have a higher purpose, be an optimist, don't wear feelings on your sleeve, and be a high-affirmation leader. If teams are energized, they are more likely to get results.

These are four of the tools we use to drive results at our company, but your role is likely different. However, the above items provide an excellent foundation upon which any leader can build, even if the way you implement them differs from other leaders' methods.

Leaders who drive results provide clarity to their team, ensure they have the right people, invest in those people, and supply the energy needed to get the job done. Leaders who simply report results likely lack these attributes, focusing instead on how they can frame whatever results occur to their benefit.

A Word of Caution

Good outcomes don't always result from good decisions. Randomness happens. Drawing false conclusions from random success is dangerous.

It has been said that if you have an infinite number of monkeys and an infinite number of typewriters, one of those monkeys will eventually write *War and Peace*. Many leaders think that because there was a good outcome, the process or decisions that led to that outcome must have been good. Not always.

Drawing False Meaning, which is sometimes called representativeness, creates false conclusions out of random events. Just because someone gets the results they want, even for something important, does not mean that person had a results focus. There are a lot of ways we can draw incorrect conclusions from random events, so we must be aware of this trap.

For instance, our industry, recreational boating, was way over retail inventoried before COVID and was in a tough spot. But COVID created a buying environment that cleared out this inventory, bailing out those who had grossly mismanaged. Those who had not focused on the long-term results of their actions were bailed out by COVID, and in some cases looked like geniuses when their very bad activity focus was bailed out by a once-in-a-century event.

There is a saying that even a blind squirrel occasionally finds a nut. But being focused on results over activity is a paradigm that generates ongoing positive outcomes.

All Hat and No Cattle

Lots of folks excel at talking a big game. They have grand ideas, offer guaranteed solutions to your problems, and promise remarkable results. However, when it comes to delivering those promises, only a few truly walk the talk. As leaders, it is crucial to differentiate between those who are, as they say in Texas, "all hat and no cattle" and those with the mindset and determination to turn their words into tangible results.

To use another analogy, individuals who excel at creating a great impression with their words yet fail to deliver when producing results are "all sizzle and no steak." These folks may possess charisma and the ability to convince an audience of what should be done, but without the substance to back it up, their words are not worth much. As leaders, it is vital to discern between those who possess genuine substance and those who are merely skilled at saying the things we want to hear. Being someone who can back up their words with tangible results is invaluable. You must ensure your team includes people who can deliver results. At Correct Craft, we often say, "It's not how, but who."

A few years ago, a gentleman, let's call him Nate, left our company and, soon after leaving, decided he wanted to rejoin us. Nate is a good guy and would merit consideration for re-hire under the right set of circumstances. However, his strategy to get rehired, which continues still even after a few years, apparently consists of reaching out to us with reasons why he can fix any challenge we have. He was saying the right things, but also claiming a level of competence not demonstrated during his time working with us. When on our team previously, Nate was very active but achieved few results. We did not hire him back.

At Correct Craft, we highly encourage and highly respect team members who will speak up and offer new ideas or new perspectives. It is part of our culture and a core value we embrace; we call it "Highly assertive – Highly Cooperative" (more on that later). We do our best to appreciate and reward employees who are willing to speak up. But people who didn't speak up until after they left? Not so much.

While it is easy to talk about what should be done, true value lies in delivering actual results. Talk is cheap; it is the results we deliver that truly matter.

Sharing Nate's story recently with two of our very high-potential leaders, who were visiting our corporate headquarters in Orlando, was important to us because they needed to understand that it is easy to talk about what should be done. Still, we need leaders to deliver actual results. We wanted them to understand that while they have a bright future, their future will not be determined based on what they say but on the results they deliver.

In the pursuit of results, mindset plays a pivotal role. It is not enough to dream, plan, and discuss ideas without taking concrete actions to bring the results to fruition. Those who achieve remarkable feats are not simply talkers; they are doers. They understand that mere effort or activity does not guarantee success. Instead, they prioritize delivering results, doing the necessary work, and going the extra mile to make things happen. It is this mindset of results that sets them apart from the rest.

To foster a culture of accountability and excellence, it is essential to focus not on rewarding effort or activity but on celebrating and rewarding tangible results. Results should always take precedence over empty promises or superficial actions. We often talk about being a "fighter pilot" (more on that later, too). Just as a fighter pilot makes calculated decisions based on real-time information, leaders must assess individuals based on their track record of achievement rather than their ability to speak convincingly. By emphasizing results, we create an environment encouraging action and holding individuals accountable for their contributions.

Avoid Monday Morning Quarterbacking

One of the pitfalls many people fall into is using hindsight to critique and analyze decisions made by others, which is often called Monday morning quarterbacking. It feels good to be right after the fact, pointing out what should have been done differently. However, true leaders understand that dwelling on the past and engaging in endless speculation does not lead to progress. Instead, even though it's riskier, they focus on the present, making informed decisions and taking immediate action to drive positive outcomes. While we should learn from the past, particularly our own mistakes, we should avoid the trap of

Monday morning quarterbacking, especially when we play the expert without understanding the situation or feeling the game-day pressure.

Planning

While action is essential, it must be coupled with good strategic planning. Leaders who achieve meaningful results understand the value of setting clear goals, creating actionable plans, and executing them diligently. They don't rely solely on the power of spontaneity or reactiveness; instead, they combine these attributes with a structured approach that aligns their actions with a strategic vision. By marrying action with thoughtful planning, leaders can navigate challenges more effectively and achieve sustainable success.

Deliver Results

In a world where talk is abundant and results are scarce, leaders must rise above the noise and demonstrate their ability to deliver. We must shift our focus from empty promises and impressive conjectures to concrete actions and tangible outcomes. By adopting a results-oriented mindset, rewarding results over activity, avoiding the trap of Monday morning quarterbacking, and requiring substance over sizzle, leaders can create a culture that values and celebrates those who transform ideas into reality.

A Message to Garcia

The very short book, *A Message to Garcia,* tells the inspiring story of a soldier who overcame tough odds to accomplish his mission in Cuba just before the Spanish-American War. Richard Clarke, a recently retired 4-Star general, asked everyone in his charge to read it. Check it out for some motivation to be more results-focused.

The best leaders don't just talk about what can be done; they deliver results. It is the doers, not the talkers, who leave a lasting impact on their organizations and the world around them. Be a doer.

Diving for a T-shirt

One of our favorite illustrations comes from a family vacation. Years ago, Bill and his family spent a wonderful week in Nevada cruising Lake Mead on a 60-foot houseboat. Bill's kids still look back on that trip as one of their favorite all-time vacations.

During that trip, Bill woke up one morning to notice one of his daughter Amanda's t-shirts had fallen off the rail, where it had been left overnight to dry. And was resting in twenty feet of crystal clear water. The first one awake to notice the submerged shirt, Bill decided he was going to get it off the lake bottom and made six or seven unsuccessful dives to get it. As Bill was diving for the t-shirt, Erin, Bill's other daughter, came out to the boat deck and asked what he was doing. Seeing his challenge, Erin made one dive and got the shirt, making it look easy. While Bill's attempts were well-intentioned, it was Erin who got the desired result. Bill had activity. Erin got results.

7 Habits of Highly Effective People

One of the best and highest-selling books of all time is Stephen Covey's *7 Habits of Highly Effective People*. It is a book we both often recommend. One of Covey's 7 Habits is "Begin with the End in Mind." That's a focus on results!

Chapter 4 Summary

- Many people tie their identity to feeling busy.
- The most effective leaders prioritize results over activity.
- Results-focused leaders avoid swirling.
- Clarity of expectations is essential for driving results.
- Reporting good results is not driving good results.
- Getting good results is sometimes random.

Who, Not How

The mess Bill inherited when he arrived at Correct Craft in 2006 is well documented. Correct Craft's primary business, Nautique Boats, was losing money and in an expensive new facility. Leadership turnover was high, distributors were dissatisfied, and morale was low. There were plenty of problems at Nautique, but none was hurting us more than lackluster product. Recent product introductions had not gone well, and there was nothing exciting in the pipeline. As a result, unfortunately, both margins and market share were declining.

Greg Meloon Moves to Orlando

Within weeks of joining Correct Craft, Bill had the opportunity to spend time with one of the company's sales representatives, a young guy based in the Midwest, Greg Meloon. Greg's great-grandfather had founded Correct Craft. It wasn't long before Bill asked Greg to leave his midwestern sales role and move to Orlando, Florida.

Once there, Greg quickly engaged in improving our product offering. Before long, new products rolled off the assembly line, and since then, not only has Nautique's market share significantly increased, but any unbiased observer would agree that the quality of their boats is second to none.

Greg was the right person at the right time. Since then, he has worked his way up the ranks and now serves as president of Nautique, Correct Craft's largest subsidiary.

When we have a problem to solve at Correct Craft, the answer is always "Who, Not How." Greg is a good example of that.

Some Other *Whos*

- At the end of 1986, the Manchester United football (known as soccer in the United States) team had been in a 20-year drought, and its rivals were dominating them. Fortunately for Manchester United, Sir Alex Ferguson took the helm. In the years that followed, Ferguson was willing to terminate senior players with bad habits and invest in both a new culture and a youth feeder system that developed players like David Beckham. Ferguson's success is indisputable, and he turned Manchester United into one of the world's most successful and valuable sports franchises.
- In 1997, Apple was rudderless, losing money, and on the edge of bankruptcy. Fortunately for the company, co-founder Steve Jobs returned to the helm. And when he returned, Jobs was bold. He was not afraid to make difficult but necessary cuts while also investing heavily in market-driving products. Jobs had a huge positive impact on Apple, and by 2011, the company was not only highly admired but also the most valuable company in the world.
- By 2014, Microsoft had lost its luster. The company had a lot of problems, made bad investments, and introduced uninspiring products. Fortunately, they found the right Who in their new CEO, Satya Nadella. Nadella upgraded products, transitioned to a cloud focus, and invested in artificial intelligence. As in the Apple story, under Nadella's leadership, Microsoft significantly improved its reputation and has since 2014, frequently been recognized as the world's most valuable company.

These are just a few of the innumerable examples. When an organization gets the right *Who* in place, extraordinary things happen.

Many Are Better Than We Are

We both have accounting backgrounds and are arguably proficient in financial management. However, with nearly 2,000 team members at Correct Craft, there is little doubt that each of them can do their job better than either of us could. Fortunately, we both understand that to be successful, we need to be on a great team. We also understand that if we have had any success, it is because of the people around us. Knowing this, whenever there is a problem to solve, we always think, "who, not how."

We often hear from leaders outside of Correct Craft who come to us asking for advice because they have problems and are unsure of what to do. When we respond, "think Who, Not How," their eyes light up as they realize the power of this idea, and they look like a big burden has been lifted.

This concept of "Who, Not How" is transformative. For leaders willing to embrace this mindset, the following five ideas will change your world for the better.

1. The Right *Who* Fixes Your Problem

When Bill asked Greg Meloon, then a Midwest sales rep for Nautique, to move to Orlando and take over product development, results came quickly; product immediately started improving. The changes Greg made were foundational to our company's turnaround and positioned us to grow Correct Craft in the years ahead. The right "Who" fixed the problem.

2. The Right *Who* Is More Than Just Competent

When Correct Craft acquired Centurion and Supreme Boats several years ago, the brands were in a similar condition as Nautique was when Bill arrived. The Centurion and Supreme brands had not fully recovered from the Great Recession and were struggling to survive.

A big challenge related to these brands was that they were based in California, a long way from our Florida headquarters.

We wanted to invest time in the company, and for a while, one of our team members was flying to California every week, but doing so was not sustainable. We needed a Who. Fortunately, Paul Singer, an experienced industry veteran, was willing to join our team and led a dramatic turnaround of Centurion and Supreme. Their revenue has grown nearly 5X, and the brands are now successful in just about every way. Paul is highly competent, but it was not just his competence that resulted in the turnaround. His character and chemistry changed the organization's culture and drove great results.

Happily, we hired the right person in Paul, but in other cases, we were not as fortunate. The one consistent mistake many leaders make over their career (we know we have) is thinking they hired the right person because the person was highly competent. Even if they are highly competent, not focusing enough on their character and chemistry always ends up in a mess. That means you probably did not get the right Who.

The right Who will have more than mere competency.

3. The Right *Who* Does Not Cost Money

When leaders view their people as an expense, they are heading down a destructive path. The right Who is never an expense; they are an investment that results in a great return. If you see your key teammates as an expense, you either have the wrong mindset or the wrong people.

At Correct Craft, we spend a tremendous amount of money on employee development. We have helped dozens of employees get their MBAs, and innumerable others have earned other degrees, certifications, or taken training with our help. Currently, we have hundreds of our team members enrolled in Correct Craft University, one of our educational development tools. We are happy to invest in our team, because we don't see them as an expense; they are people we care about and are valuable investments.

4. The Right *Who* Loves To Help

Sometimes leaders will feel bad about asking others to do work they don't want to do. If that's you, shake that thinking. Finding the right Who is not a matter of getting someone to do what you don't like. Finding the right Who is a matter of providing someone an opportunity to do something at which they excel and enjoy.

We are all wired differently, and that is a foundation of teamwork. What de-energizes you is likely to seriously energize someone else. Leaders have a responsibility to energize their organization; finding the right Who for each job is a great way to do that.

5. The Wrong *Who* Must Leave the Team

Over the years, we have occasionally found ourselves in the unenviable position of needing to terminate a teammate, sometimes even someone we really like. It is always hard. We try to provide a high-care environment at Correct Craft, so making people changes is always challenging. However, when the wrong Who is on the team, a leader must be willing to make the necessary change. Dr. Henry Cloud writes about this in *Necessary Endings,* a book that has profoundly affected our team's thinking.

A Transformative Concept

Many leaders spend years trying to find the solution to a problem and will keep spending time on the problem if they must figure it out themselves. Finding the right Who solves problems more quickly and creates a lot of additional time for the leader to focus on areas where they excel.

This is a transformative concept that can change the trajectory of your company and career.

For those who want to learn more, we highly recommend the book *Who Not How* by Dan Sullivan and Benjamin Hardy.

Thinking "Who, not How" has positively affected Correct Craft, and we are certain it can help you too.

In the next chapter we will consider an important path of identifying the right who: character, competence, and chemistry.

Chapter 5: Summary

- When a leader is considering how to solve a problem, they should think "Who, Not How."
- There are many examples of the right Who transforming an organization.
- The right Who:
    1. Fixes your problem.
    2. Is more than just competent.
    3. Does not cost money.
    4. Loves to help.
- The wrong Who must leave the team.

Character, Competence, Chemistry

One of Bill's biggest challenges in his early days at Correct Craft was related to boat production. The company was in the middle of a major transition, moving from Correct Craft's historical batch boat building to a new linear assembly process. This production change was driven by the move to a new facility a few months earlier, and it was far from smooth.

To make matters more difficult, Bill arrived right after the company lost two key leaders. His predecessor had deep experience in production management, but he had gone back to his former job. And the gentleman who had led the Correct Craft boat production for decades died of a heart attack not long before Bill arrived. Bill did not have much experience in small-boat production; he knew that he needed help, and he needed it fast. So, he started searching for a new boat builder.

Looking for a New Production Leader

Bill launched an urgent search for a new production leader. After weeks of searching for the new person and interviewing candidates, he found an incredibly talented production leader, whom we will call Larry. Larry was well credentialed and had experience that made him an obvious, highly competent candidate. Bill was confident he had found the right candidate and hired Larry to take over production at Correct Craft.

Larry made an immediate and significant impact. He was making difficult changes that were needed and set the organization on the path of building better boats. Yet, about three months into his tenure with Correct Craft, Bill made the difficult decision to fire him. It was tough, but necessary.

Larry was highly competent, but he lacked the character and chemistry Bill was working to build into Correct Craft's culture. It was a seminal moment of Bill's tenure as Correct Craft's new CEO because, as much as he needed Larry's competence, he was also very intentional about building a great culture of "Making Life Better" based on people, performance, and philanthropy. Larry was competent, but he didn't fit.

A very similar situation occurred a couple of years later when Bill reorganized how the company managed its international sales. Once again, Bill hired a highly competent international sales leader, but the gentleman did not have the character and chemistry that had become a non-negotiable for the Correct Craft team. Despite this gentleman's demonstrated competency, again, a tough change was made.

A Confession

OK, Bill is writing this confession paragraph. I will admit that the single biggest and most consistent mistake I have made over my career is hiring for competency and not paying enough attention to character and chemistry. I would never knowingly hire someone with inadequate character or chemistry, but I can get emotionally hijacked by a candidate's competency and not focus enough on their character and chemistry during the interview process. When someone appears capable of solving an urgent problem, it can be easy to overlook the warning signs. And I always regret it.

Over my career, this mistake on my part has resulted in me asking some very competent people to leave organizations I have led. That is not good for the organization and often deeply upsets the people I have asked to leave. One good result is that in almost every case, the person I have asked to leave has found another great opportunity, usually one that fits them better.

Why Does This Happen?

When leaders have a problem to be solved and believe they have found someone who has the competence to solve that problem, it is easy to be blinded to any reason that would indicate they should not hire the candidate. Leaders, like Bill, can forget a valuable hiring mindset that has been an important part of Correct Craft's success. That mindset always considers character, competency, and chemistry when hiring; all three are necessary.

What Must Be Done

Leaders must hire for character, competence, and chemistry, and not get hijacked by just one of these attributes, no matter how compelling it may be. Unfortunately, it is easy to become captured by any one of these attributes in a candidate, and when that happens, it is usually bad. When hiring, leaders must have a mindset that all three are required before bringing someone new onto their team. All three are essential.

Some Background

The triad of character, competence, and chemistry has been utilized for decades by leaders and organizations for hiring and employee evaluations. But its roots actually date back to Aristotle. He described these three attributes as ethos, logos, and pathos. Whether looking at them from an English or a Greek perspective, they are powerful concepts. While we are not sure who was first to use this triad in modern times, it has developed over decades of use in psychology, leadership, and sports.

Character

Character refers to integrity. It reflects a person's willingness to set aside personal interests for the good of a group. People with character base their lives on core principles for which they are willing to sacrifice. Character can be evaluated by examining either how a person has historically reacted in difficult situations or how they act when they can get away with doing something that would seemingly violate their stated values.

Peter Drucker was one of the first management gurus to heavily emphasize character in hiring. He is reported to have said, "Hire for character first; everything else is trainable." Jim Collins, author of *Good to Great*, echoed this sentiment, emphasizing character and a specific part of character, humility. Another important leadership thinker, Stephen Covey, made character an essential part of his teaching.

One more author we respect is Pat Lencioni. His book *Five Dysfunctions of a Team* is probably the single best book on team effectiveness. The foundation for Lencioni's framework is trust, and when reading his book, you quickly realize that an effective team cannot be built without it. And earning trust requires character.

A good sign of character is a leader who has strong values, with integrity and trustworthiness to live them out. Some would argue (though we believe all three are equally important) that character is the most important of the three attributes: character, competence, and chemistry. **One thing we know for sure, a leader with competence and chemistry, but little character, is dangerous.**

Competence

Competence is a person's ability to do their job. It can be evaluated by education, certification, skill, ability, experience, and demonstrated performance. Many people evaluate competence based on the ability to solve a problem or achieve a goal.

We learn from Peter Drucker that competence is demonstrated by consistently producing required results to an agreed-upon standard. When you are reviewing competence, the easiest way is to consider whether the person you are interviewing can do the job. Or, more importantly, can they do the job under pressure?

Of the three attributes, competence is the easiest to assess.

Chemistry

Chemistry refers to how well a person gets along with and works with others. The importance of chemistry gained widespread attention in the sports world with coaches such as John Wooden, Bill Walsh, and Phil Jackson. In time, the importance of building chemistry in sports with clear success raised awareness of its benefits among business leaders and organizational psychologists. Today, almost everyone agrees that effective chemistry is needed for a well-run team.

Chemistry looks different for every team but can be generally defined as working well with teammates, cultural fit, and interpersonal effectiveness. Some people have natural chemistry, while others are naturally reserved which can sometimes be mistaken for lack of chemistry.

Many of the best leaders will use temperament assessments (i.e., Myers-Briggs, DISC, Predictive Index, Working Genius) to help their team better understand themselves and each other. Information is readily available on each of these assessment tools, so we won't share much more regarding them, other than to note that these tools have all been incredibly helpful at Correct Craft and have made our teams stronger. We have participated in many teambuilding sessions using these tools and are always amazed at how much people learn about themselves and each other in those classes.

Every leader should review and draw their own conclusions regarding the effectiveness of assessments. But we can say without qualification that these tools have significantly helped our Correct Craft team understand more about ourselves and each other. We are a better team because of them.

There has been much written about chemistry, and why it is so hard to develop among teams. But the root cause of chemistry issues generally connects back to one of three problems: putting tasks over people, not understanding your teammates, or a lack of self-awareness. Often all three are factors.

What's the Most Important?

Many leaders want to rank character, chemistry, and competency. We would caution leaders against doing that. Character, competence, and chemistry are all essential, but none is sufficient on their own. However, when you find someone with all three, everything is easier.

An Example of All Three

A powerful example comes from Correct Craft's experience harmonizing our enterprise resource planning (ERP) systems. Because of Correct Craft's acquisitions over several years, we ended up with several different companies with diverse ERP systems. We knew these systems needed to be harmonized across our company, but it seemed like a huge job. Almost anyone who has been through an ERP changeover can attest to how difficult they are. We didn't have just one system to change: we had several.

We had plenty of reasons to put off this harmonization, but a few years ago, Bill decided Correct Craft needed to get this done before he stepped down as CEO. He didn't want to leave the problem for Correct Craft's next CEO, but he was also dreading the challenges and maybe even chaos the harmonization would likely create for the organization.

Remarkably, the ERP harmonization went extremely well. It was hard work, and there was some frustration during the change. However, there was much more talk among our folks about the benefits of the new system than the challenges related to changing it.

We had never experienced, or even heard of, an ERP transition going as well as ours did. It was all made possible because our Chief Operating Officer, Angela Pilkington, put together an implementation team that had all three of the attributes we are discussing in this chapter: character, competence, and chemistry. That mindset in choosing the ERP implementation team saved our Correct Craft employees a lot of frustration and likely saved the company millions of dollars.

Conclusion

Focusing on character, chemistry, and competence provides a leader with the best framework to evaluate current and prospective team members and make sure the right folks are on board.

The best teammates have all three characteristics: character, competence, and chemistry. As we wrote in the last chapter, "Who, Not How," when you find the right person, your problems go away.

We have seen the benefits of a mindset that focuses on character, competence, and chemistry, and experienced the challenges of not having that mindset. Speaking from experience, having the mindset we encourage in this chapter works in a big way.

In the next chapter, we will discuss why it's important that everyone on your team is willing to speak up.

Chapter 6 Summary

- The best teams are built on people who have character, competence, and chemistry.
- Leaders, when hiring, can get captured by one of these three attributes that a candidate expresses well and do not pay enough attention to the other two. This is a big mistake.
- Character, competence, and chemistry are all essential but never sufficient on their own.
- We have seen firsthand the huge benefit of a mindset that gives importance to character, competency, and chemistry in choosing team members.

Chapter 7

Don't be a Silent Liar

Years before joining Correct Craft, Zach worked on the finance team of a major theme park in Central Florida. Being early in his career, he had little experience and a lot to learn. One day, he was invited to a meeting with the park's senior leaders to discuss a new piece of equipment for his department. This equipment was used to count and sort cash and was fully integrated with the latest technology. This was a large purchase, and this capital investment was intended to improve efficiency, accuracy, and output for his team.

The leaders in the meeting ranked quite a bit above him in the chain of command, so Zach viewed this as an opportunity to learn. During the meeting, his boss laid out the current challenges with the old equipment, shared the bells and whistles included on the new equipment, and explained why investing in this equipment will be a win for the company. This seemed to make sense to the rest of the people in the room, as they all nodded in agreement to offer support.

While on the surface this made sense, Zach knew the details of the work, and knew this equipment wasn't suitable for the actual work to be done. There were nuisances to the work that this equipment couldn't handle, and without addressing these up front, the project was going to fail.

While Zach knew this, he was also the most junior person in the room, so he didn't speak up. Unfortunately, the concerns Zach had about the equipment were right and ended up causing a big head- ache for him and his teammates.

By not speaking up and sharing his concerns during the meeting, Zach was what we call a "silent liar."

Highly Assertive/ Highly Cooperative

If you've been in a meeting at Correct Craft, especially one where a new idea, product, or plan is being discussed, chances are you've heard collaboration, a lot of discussion, and even friendly debate about the topic of focus. We are thrilled about that!

In the following excerpt from *Making Life Better: The Correct Craft Story,* Bill shares how the culture that has been built at Correct Craft allows for this:

> *"We've worked hard to foster a unique, high-trust culture that encourages open communication and different perspectives. As a result, politics are almost non-existent, and the group puts the team, our products, and brands above the individual.*
>
> *In order to make life better, we know we need a culture of excellence that values everyone in the organization and seeks input from each team member. We still have high expectations and hold people accountable for their results, but they are much more likely to want to produce in the right environment, knowing their input matters to their leaders.*
>
> *We also know that not every idea is always the best idea, so it's important to have a variety of perspectives. For this to happen, employees must feel that they can be open and honest. Over the years I've found that this highly assertive, highly cooperative environment encourages people to speak up and share ideas to make our company better."*

No Silent Liars

An important part of this highly assertive, highly cooperative environment at Correct Craft is the concept of no silent liars. A silent liar is someone who has an idea or opinion and instead of sharing it, decides to keep it to themselves. In some instances, we may say something, and one of our team members may think, "Whoa, that's the craziest thing I've ever heard." Or, other times, they may think, "I don't think they have all the facts." If that happens, we want our team to speak up; we want to hear everyone's ideas. While we want everyone to speak up, it's best to do so with respect and manners; this is not an excuse to be a jerk. But we don't want a team member to be a silent liar.

So, Why Don't People Speak Up?

One of the most common reasons employees don't speak up in a meeting is a lack of trust. Effective teams require trust; without it, everything else breaks down. Patrick Lencioni writes about this in his book *The Five Dysfunctions of a Team,* where he identifies trust as the foundation of teamwork and the most critical piece of building a team. According to Lencioni, trust is the foundational principle of team cohesiveness.

Trust within a team is demonstrated when everyone feels comfortable speaking up and is confident that those in the room want the best for them. In other words, no one is holding a dagger behind their back waiting to strike. They are willing to share their ideas freely, even when those ideas are counter to the consensus.

Another effective way to encourage employees to speak up is for leaders to be the last to share their opinions.

Correct Craft is Different

A few years ago, Shane Stanfill joined the Correct Craft team to lead one of our new companies. He was a seasoned leader with a lot of industry experience and a great culture fit. He had worked for other well-known companies in the industry and had experienced firsthand an environment that lacked trust and vulnerability.

After Shane's first Correct Craft board meeting, he had the opportunity to share some of the great results his new team was achieving. Shane came up to Zach and said, "Wow, this was so much different than other board meetings I have been to. In my past, board meetings were used to highlight individual successes by tearing down the others around you." Shane continues to be a great leader today, building high-trust, high-performance teams.

Unfortunately, trust may take a long time to develop. To shortcut that process, we tell our teams we should not make people earn our trust; instead, we give trust until it is violated. This concept alone can shorten the time for gaining team effectiveness by months or years.

How a Leader Responds Matters

Leaders must model the values they have identified as important. As senior leaders at Correct Craft, we know that if we don't listen carefully to opinions that are contrary to ours and respect the team member who opened up, it will be the last time they or anyone else in the meeting will speak up.

Respect for People Who Will Speak Up

During high school, Zach got his first job working at a local restaurant that had just opened. He worked in the kitchen and also helped as a food runner, taking food to customers' tables. The kitchen manager, whom we will call Sam, had worked in the food industry for a long time and was not the nicest boss to Zach or anyone else.

One day, during a pre-opening team meeting, Sam discussed with the staff the prep work needed for the day. He was assigning cleaning tasks, asking for updates on various inventory levels, and reviewing menu specials with the waiters. As Sam was going through the daily specials, Suzy, one of the waitresses, suggested a different way to prepare the plate based on customer feedback. Sam's immediate response to her was, "You aren't paid to be the chef, stick with being a waitress." In that moment, everyone froze, and it was the last time anyone spoke up in a team meeting. Poor Suzy, who was a good employee, didn't work there much longer. Sam's response to Suzy cost the company in several different ways.

Being a leader does not exempt you from the values you say are important; in fact, you must submit to them more than anyone.

Respecting someone's opinion does not mean you have to agree with it; we know not all ideas are good ones. In fact, in a highly collaborative environment, most ideas aren't fully thought through. What matters is listening and responding with appreciation and explanation. We honor those who resist being silent liars because we know it makes the team better.

Stanford Design Thinking

In 2023, Zach took a course at the Stanford "d. school" on design thinking. Design thinking is a human-centered approach to solving complex problems that emphasizes learning through making.

One of the fundamentals of design thinking is the concept of divergent and convergent thinking. Divergent thinking is the process of generating a wide range of possible solutions from diverse perspectives. You want to embrace creativity and refrain from judgment. Convergent thinking is when you start synthesizing patterns and insights to narrow down to a few good ideas.

To demonstrate this concept during the course, the students were placed into groups, given sticky notes and a vague problem, and then given five minutes to come up with as many possible solutions as possible. Zach and his team began writing quickly and putting as many ideas on the wall as possible. When time expired, they grouped the ideas into common themes and selected which ones to move forward. They also enjoyed laughing at some of the stray ideas that made it up on the wall.

What Zach and his fellow students found was that the more ideas that were generated during the divergent thinking process, the better the final project.

The same is true for teams at work. Not all ideas make it through the final cut, but we still value the role they play in shaping the final decision. We need people to speak up.

How Do You Know if Someone is a Silent Liar?

Sometimes, no matter how open a leader is to feedback, someone on the team is being a silent liar. In smaller groups, it is easier to identify when someone is being a silent liar, but it's not always obvious. Below are key signs of someone being a silent liar.

- Disengaged – not participating or sharing their thoughts
- Body language – cold or intimidated, visible negative facial expressions

If someone is demonstrating signs of disagreement, it may be appropriate to solicit their input directly. Saying something like, "Jane, I always value your input. Do you have any thoughts about this?" is a good way to gain their perspective. Or if they are demonstrating negative body language, you could say, "John, you look like you see this differently. I'd really appreciate hearing your perspective." Showing your appreciation for their input is usually the best way to energize team members to speak up and help them avoid being a silent liar.

Highly Cooperative

Just as important as it is to speak up, there comes a time when a decision has to be made, and the group has to rally around that decision.

Run the Play Called

Imagine you are on a football team, and you are in the huddle, listening for the next play. In the huddle, the tight end recommends running a short pass play and the wide receiver recommends a deep ball. Before the huddle breaks, the quarterback calls a play for the wide receiver to run a slant route and to catch the ball 15 yards down the field. The huddle breaks, the players line up, and the quarterback yells, "Hike!" As the play unfolds, the tight end and wide receiver both decide to run the play they recommended, causing the original slant route play to fall apart. After the play is over, they say, "See, I told you that play wasn't going to work." Unfortunately for them, the play's failure also means they are off the field, as the defense has to go to work.

Just as important as it is for the football players to run the right play, it is important for a team to understand the decision and run the play that is called. Every team must do everything they can to make the play successful.

People will sometimes run their own play when they get hijacked by the perceived rightness of their own idea, and therefore can't emotionally separate from it. They will find ways to circle back, discuss what has already been discussed, or be overly negative towards others in an effort to push for their idea. This can cause frustration for the rest of the group as the conversation continues to swirl. Chapter 10 discusses ways to overcome swirling, so keep reading!

If you find yourself getting emotionally attached to an idea that is not chosen, it is important to take a step back, ensure you are heard and understood, and then respect the decision that is made.

Avoid Shadow Missions

A culture absent of trust, with minimal collaboration, and where employees don't feel respected, can lead to shadow missions. A shadow mission is when the goal people act towards, or the behavior of the team, is different than the stated or intended goal. In other words, it's when you say one thing publicly, but act in a different way.

Common examples of shadow missions are:

- Stated Goal: Collaborate across the organization
  Shadow Mission: Protect your project
- Stated Goal: Reward based on results
  Shadow Mission: Reward hard work
- Stated Goal: Invest in innovation
  Shadow Mission: Failure is unacceptable

Shadow missions are dangerous because they can cause confusion and cynicism and ultimately undermine the success of the organization.

It's important to identify and correct shadow missions quickly, before they have an opportunity to grow roots deep within the organization. To do this, we work hard to foster a culture that encourages our team to not be silent liars and share their diverse perspectives to make our company better.

The best teams do all they can to provide a safe environment so employees won't become silent liars. This isn't always easy, but we'll learn more in the next chapter about doing the hard things.

Chapter 7 Summary

- A silent liar is someone who has an idea or opinion, but instead of sharing decides to keep it to themselves.
- Not every idea is the best idea, so it's good to have diverse perspectives.
- How a leader responds matters.
- After a decision is made, everyone has to run the same play.
- Watch out for shadow missions.

Do the Hard Things

The Big Sur International Marathon is known for its challenging terrain, significant elevation changes, and the infamous "Hurricane Point" from miles ten to twelve, where runners face strong winds while they grind up a two-mile ascent. After reaching the highest elevation point, the iconic Bixby Creek Bridge is there to greet you, followed by another thirteen miles of rolling coastal terrain. It is tough!

Zach faced this in 2019 when he ran the Big Sur Marathon for the first time. Living in Florida left him with limited opportunities to train for the type of race he signed up for, yet somehow, he was able to set a new personal best marathon time in one of the United States's most challenging races. So, what was the game-changer for his training? Being willing to embrace the challenge of doing hard things.

Accept Discomfort

The pressure of leadership is real, and it's not something easily understood until you are in the position. Leaders face moments where decisions carry real consequences, and the weight of responsibility cannot be delegated to anyone else. This can be hard, but great leaders have the mindset to do the hard things.

During an early morning training run, Zach was talking with Daniel, a seasoned elite marathoner, about the late-mile pain of a marathon. Through the conversation Daniel shared with Zach, some advice that fundamentally changed his mindset: "You know it will be uncomfortable, so be okay with that." As elite marathoner Kenenisa Bekele once said, "The difference between a champion and the rest is who pushes through the hardest moments."

Running a marathon is no easy task, but when you choose to accept discomfort and push through the most challenging moments, you can unlock another level of performance. The same is true for business leaders. We reach new heights when we do the hard things.

And the best leaders are willing to do the hard things. The short run may be more difficult, but the long run will be better.

In fact, because Zach learned to embrace discomfort during marathon training, he was able to enjoy the incredible views of Big Sur and the Pacific Ocean.

So, what are some of the hard things leaders face?

Dealing with Big Rocks

Sometimes leaders know what needs to be done, but the project is so daunting that it gets postponed indefinitely. This happens all the time in business, especially during periods of rapid growth. Paul Singer, the former president of Centurion and Supreme boats, used to call these "Big Rocks."

Correct Craft has grown significantly, with annual revenue increasing from ~$39 million in 2009 to $1 billion plus in 2023. During that period of rapid growth, we started realizing that our Human Resources Information System (HRIS) wasn't keeping up with our needs. We knew there were better systems out there, but dreaded going through the pain of making a switch. This impacted people's paychecks, and nobody wants to be responsible for our team not getting paid.

Thankfully, Jodie Haven MacLean, Correct Craft's Chief Administrative Officer, is a leader who is willing to do the hard things. Jodie and her amazing team put a plan together and dealt with this big rock.

Because of the planning and hard work the team put in, the project has gone smoothly, And impressively, it has energized the team as they begin seeing the benefits of the relentless effort. Good leaders are willing to do hard things and deal with the big rocks, as they are often the limiters of growth. If Jodie had avoided doing this hard thing, it would have seriously impeded Correct Craft's ability to grow.

It's Always Been Done This Way

One of the most frustrating answers for why a task is done a certain way, or even done at all, is "because it's always been done this way." Who hasn't heard this before?

Sometimes we become complacent with a legacy project, product, or event, even after the original purpose becomes obsolete or irrelevant. This happens as customer interests change, the market shifts, or technology advances.

At Correct Craft, we want to be market-driving, not market-driven. While we use market and industry research as reference points, we've found that market research can be notoriously wrong. Instead, we want to develop products that the industry doesn't even know it wants yet (think iPad!). To do this, we have to be willing to do the hard things, break away from the way it has always been done, and challenge the status quo. Next time you hear someone say, "It's always been done this way," that's a good time to ask more questions!

Necessary Endings

Some of the most difficult challenges leaders face involve people. No matter how hard we try to make relationships work, sometimes it's best for us, and often for them, to go separate ways. This is true with employees, vendors, distributors, and partners.

Henry Cloud's book *Necessary Endings* helped our Correct Craft team be more effective in this area. We are wired to care about people, and none of us enjoys having to make a necessary ending. In fact, often the feedback we hear from our teams is we take too long to make an essential change.

However, in our experience, failure to end what isn't working is one of the primary reasons organizations get stuck. Endings create the space, the energy, and the momentum for better things to begin.

So why are endings so hard? Often, necessary endings are avoided because:

- The person has a unique technical ability that is hard to replace.
- There is a fear of conflict.
- Guilt or compassion.
- There is a hope for change.

When a challenging person who brings others down is also an underperformer, the decision is simple: you let them go. Unfortunately, that's not always the case. More often, leaders will tolerate poor behavior when that person has a unique skill set the organization fears losing. That fear can be paralyzing, but it also has long term negative effects on the team.

If poor behavior by higher performers is tolerated, several things happen within the organization.

- Culture erodes.
- Trust breaks down.
- The good people leave.
- Silos are built within the organization.

So, if someone on your team consistently:

- Disrespects others.
- Undermines the team or company.
- Lives by a separate set of standards.
- Ignores or refuses feedback.
- Repeats the same behavioral issues.

Then it is time to do a hard thing and consider a necessary ending, even if that person is a high performer.

Hard on the Problem, Soft on the People

Have you ever offered logical, constructive feedback in a meeting only to be met with an unexpectedly emotional response? The reason lies in how the brain works.

The human brain is the body's central command center, controlling our thoughts, memory, emotions, reactions, movements, senses, and breathing functions. Even the world's most advanced computers don't come close to replicating the computing power of one human brain.

One of the most fascinating brain functions is the brain's response to perceived dangers, often called the fight-or-flight response. This response occurs when the brain's amygdala identifies a perceived threat, triggering the hypothalamus to activate the sympathetic nervous system and flooding your body with adrenaline and cortisol for immediate action.

When this happens, the brain bypasses the prefrontal cortex, the part of the brain responsible for logical and rational reasoning, to prepare you to confront or escape the threat.

Essentially, this means that when a person feels personally threatened or attacked, even if that threat is emotional, their brain is wired to ignore logical reasoning. They will often respond in one of two ways, either with high intensity, fueled with anger, or by shutting down, not responding, and escaping the situation. Either way, that person is not listening or processing information in a logical manner.

Correct Craft is filled with wonderful people, but sometimes as leaders we are faced with having difficult conversations. Keeping in mind the brain's scientific wiring, when having a difficult conversation, it is important to show respect toward the person while clearly addressing the behavior or actions of concern. At Correct Craft, we call this being hard on the problem, while soft on the person.

Be Confident in your Decision, Courageous in your Actions

After graduating from college, Zach worked at an Orlando theme park managing the park's cash vault operations. The cash vault team was responsible for counting all cash generated in the park the day before and preparing the cash registers with a standard assortment of change to open the next day. This was back when most people actually paid with cash.

There was a team of eight employees whom Zach was responsible for leading, and every person was vitally important to the day's work getting done. If one person called in sick, the additional workload fell on the rest of the team to complete—something the team was willing to do, to a point.

One of the cash vault employees, let's call her Stephanie, was a very nice young lady, but she struggled to arrive at work on time. Most of the time there was an excuse: her car broke down, or her alarm didn't go off. However, at other times she just didn't show up. After repeated conversations, written warnings, and plenty of opportunities to correct the behavior, it was time for Zach to make a necessary ending with Stephanie.

This role was Zach's first opportunity to manage a team, and no matter how justified the decision, it was no fun to let Stephanie go. Zach knew it meant calling her into an office with a Human Resources manager, walking her through the circumstances that brought them there, and finally letting her know the decision that was made. This was really going to be a hard day.

While preparing for the meeting, Zach called someone he knew he could trust, his dad, looking for some advice on how to go about this. The advice he got has stuck with him ever since, "Zach, no matter how hard this day is for you, it's 10x harder for her. Be kind, confident in your decision, and courageous in your actions." Wow – this provided so much clarity.

When preparing for a hard conversation, it is important to be confident in the decision you are making. Start by asking yourself a couple of simple questions. First, what are my values, and does the behavior I'm addressing fall outside of those values? Second, have I been clear about my expectations? And has the person been given every opportunity to succeed?

The final step is to have courage. Take a deep breath, prepare yourself mentally, eliminate high emotion, and take action. Remember, as hard as it is for you, it's often even harder for the person on the receiving end.

Confronting Problems

Scientists around the world have made remarkable advancements in cancer treatments.

In fact, the survival rate of many common cancers is over 90% if caught and treated early enough, whereas survival rates of advanced cancers often drops to under 20%.

The same is true when dealing with cancers within or around an organization.

Leaders often find it much easier to ignore problems, though ignoring them doesn't make them go away. Dealing with problems is hard. There is uncertainty around how people will react, and that uncertainty can be paralyzing.

However, avoiding problems allows cancer to spread within the organization, eventually destroying the positive culture you have worked so hard to build. The best leaders are willing to do the hard things and confront problems before they spread.

In our experience, problems don't go away with time. Instead, it's the complete opposite. They get worse.

This isn't the last time we will talk about doing hard things. Let's move on to Mindset #9.

Chapter 8 Summary

- The best leaders Do the Hard Things.
- Learn to embrace discomfort.
- The short run may be more challenging, but the long run will be better.
- Endings create the space, the energy, and the momentum for better things to begin.

- Be hard on the problem, soft on the person. Remember, our brains are wired to protect us from physical and emotional threats.
- Be confident in your decision, courageous in your actions.
- Good leaders are willing to deal with the big rocks, as they are often the limiters of growth.
- Problems get bigger with time.

Chapter 9

Be a Transformer

Organizations have three types of employees: maintainers, improvers, and transformers. And this fact is important: all three of these groups are not only necessary but critical for a well-run organization.

However, while every organization needs all three types of employees, our experience has shown that those who adopt a transformer mindset dramatically improve their odds of not only benefiting their organizations but also advancing their career.

Bill first introduced this framework in his book, *Education of a CEO: Lessons for* Leaders. Below is an excerpt from *Education of a CEO*.

Good Ideas Are Sometimes Born in Canada

Years ago, just before our family left for a vacation in Western Canada, I was counseling some employees on what it takes to move up the corporate ladder. Employees who show up on time every day, work hard, take part in the company development program, and have good attitudes were wondering why they were not advancing in their careers, or if they were, why it wasn't happening faster.

These employee conversations were on my mind while driving on Canadian Highway #1 from Banff to Lake Louise. Maybe it was time away from my normal routine or the beautiful scenery my family was enjoying, but while driving that mountain highway, I had a breakthrough, an epiphany. Or at least it was one for me.

Suddenly, the answer to these employee frustrations became clear. Of course, I was excited and had to share the idea with my family, which they just love me doing while we are on vacation. Actually, it doesn't excite them, but thankfully they tolerate me.

My Epiphany

It hit me that good employees fall into three categories: maintainers, improvers, and transformers. All three categories include wonderful employees who are needed by every organization, but there is one group that is most likely to move up.

Maintainers are the backbone of an organization. They include people like my father who are incredibly loyal to their teams and show up every day with the desire to work hard and do whatever is necessary for their company's success. My dad was not a corporate ladder-climber, but he was essential to his organization, a contributor who added value for thirty-five years. Dad was an incredible employee, as we learned from his co-workers when he had to go out on disability. But he had other, more important priorities than ladder-climbing, such as his family and church, and he was happy to come home to us each day at 4:30 p.m. I am very thankful for that.

Organizations cannot operate without maintainers. They are people who keep the business running. They should be treated well and with respect. Without maintainers, there is no business.

Improvers are also important to an organization; they make things better, and often, they effectively lead teams. Improvers are also imperative because they not only maintain but also help move the orga-

nization forward. Often, improvers get frustrated because they know they make things better at their organization, but don't understand why they don't make it into the top spots.

Organizations cannot operate without improvers. They work with the maintainers to ensure goals are met and exceeded. Without improvers, there is no business.

Just as the name implies, transformers are the people who significantly change things for the better. They are creative and innovative and, more importantly, ensure their team isn't just doing things right but that the team is doing the right things. In other words, transformers not only make sure the team is using the best techniques and saw to cut down the trees, but they also ensure the team is in the right forest. Transformers don't find a better way to accomplish goals; they find a different way. When transformers share great ideas, others often think about how obvious the idea is and wonder why no one else thought of it, but people often can't see the new way until the transformer points it out.

Let me say it again: Transformers don't just make things better—they make them different. Anyone from these three groups can climb the corporate ladder, but those who generally go to the top are transformers.

Organizations can operate without transformers, but they are likely in a death spiral. Maybe a slow, even imperceptible death spiral, but if an organization is not transforming, they are definitely dying.

The fact that transformers often get the top jobs can be extremely frustrating to maintainers and improvers, especially since they often do not realize what is happening. It can be particularly frustrating if they see areas where they are better or work harder than the transformer.

You might disagree with me as you read this chapter, thinking of a glaring example from your career of a maintainer or improver moving up to the top of an organization. Of course, there are examples of that. It's not that a maintainer or improver cannot move up — it's just that it is way more likely for a transformer to do so.

The business landscape is littered with organizations that have offered a great, innovative-for-the-time product but still went out of business. Kodak, Blockbuster, Nokia, Palm, and others are great examples of brands that were part of great companies and run by smart people who were making improvements. However, they did not transform and eventually went away. That is why transformers are so critical and are the most certain to advance in their careers.

For some, this idea of needing to be a transformer to advance seems unfair. They wonder why anyone who is loyal, hardworking, honest, and making the business better shouldn't advance. People with these characteristics do advance and always will. But the surest way to the top is to be a transformer.

Being a transformer is not just doing things right, it is doing the right things.

A Real-Life Transformer

If you look up the word "transformer" in my dictionary, you will see a picture of Paul Singer.

When I invited Paul to breakfast at the Black Bear Diner in Madera, California, most of what I knew about Paul came by way of his outstanding reputation in the boat business. Paul had played a huge part in building one of our industry's largest boat companies, and I was hoping to convince him to become president of our Correct Craft company in Merced, Centurion and Supreme Boats. At the time, Paul was more interested in starting a ministry at his church, but thankfully for the people he would soon be leading, he chose to see them as his ministry.

Having been involved in some significant business turnarounds, I had no doubt about the challenges Paul was taking on when he agreed to become president of our California company. I knew it would be tough and had high expectations for him; however, I had no idea what a true transformer he was. Paul totally reshaped Centurion and Supreme Boats.

Paul did all the things a new president should do when joining a company that is struggling. He improved margins, reduced expenses as a percentage of sales, built a great sales team that nearly doubled sales, invested in great new product, improved customer service, and developed a marketing program that was impactful and built brand equity. Paul would be the first to say he had an amazing team helping him, but he was leading the group and was creating an environment where all the progress was being made. Doing all of this would be enough to qualify Paul as a transformer, but honestly, it was the least of his accomplishments. Paul's biggest accomplishment was totally reshaping the culture and team at Centurion and Supreme.

Paul implemented a culture at Centurion and Supreme that dramatically impacted the lives of his team. He was transparent with the team as he gave them information regarding the improvements the company needed. By taking a personal interest in his *team members, he developed a culture of care and even started a Bible study for his team. Paul took time to work with them on service projects that improved their community. He set up a reward program for his team that now pays out more each year in employee bonuses than the company used to make in total profit. Paul cared about his team and made their lives significantly better.*

Regarding the "nuts and bolts" of the business, Paul kept doing the hard things. In fact, it was part of his constant message to the team. I often heard him say, "We have to do the hard things." Regarding the people, Paul clearly loves and is passionate about his team. He didn't just make Centurion and Supreme better; he made them different.

The Centurion and Supreme story must be one of the biggest transformations in business history—definitely in our industry. I know that sounds like hyperbole, but it is not. Paul may be the clearest transformer I have met, and as Patrick Lencioni describes it, he is the quintessential "responsibility-centered" leader.

Big and Different

The leaders who have the most impact have a transformer mindset. Their thinking is big and different, especially when big and different thinking is required.

Another Transformer – Mark McKinney

For years, Mark McKinney worked as Vice President and Chief Engineer of Correct Craft's Pleasurecraft Engine Group, builder of PCM and Crusader engines. Over three decades, he became the world's foremost expert on inboard engines. Mark was a clear transformer as an engineer who had a huge impact on products and customers all over the world.

Mark's transformer mindset as an engineer opened the door for him to grow further into leadership. Mark became Pleasurecraft Engine Group's President. As President, Mark's real transformer skills were on display. Mark was instrumental in Correct Craft forming Liberty Technologies, a propulsion technology holding company that he leads. Liberty Technologies not only included Pleasurecraft Engine Group but, under Mark's leadership, also acquired two other out-standing companies, Velvet Drive Transmissions and Indmar Engines.

As Liberty Technologies' President, Mark continued transforming products. Our company, customers, and industry will benefit from his transformative product work for a long time. He also transformed the facilities at all three companies, creating state-of-the-art production systems at each. Most importantly, under Mark's leadership, the cultures of all three Liberty Technologies' companies were transformed, and their teams embrace not only the principles of the Correct Craft Culture Pyramid but also the mindsets shared in this book.

Mark is a clear transformer, but there is an important lesson to learn from Mark's experience. The lesson is that transformers function as transformers in their current role, and that is what gives them future opportunities.

Start Where You Are

Transformers do not wait for promotions or raises to transform.

Many people have come to us over the years promising to become a transformer if promoted or given a pay raise. But that's not how it works. Transformers excel in their current role, and that is what provides them with opportunity.

Folks with career aspirations often ask us what they need to do to move up the organizational ladder. The answer is simple: the single best thing to do for your future career is to be a transformer in your current role.

Conclusion

Every organization needs maintainers, improvers, and transformers. All three matter. All three add value.

But it is the transformer mindset that is most likely to propel an organization and employees to new heights of success.

In the next chapter, we will discuss why, whatever your mindset, you must be prepared to "Get Off the X."

Chapter 9 Summary

- Maintainers keep the wheels of an organization moving forward and are critical to its success.
- Improvers are always working to make things better at their organization.
- Transformers think bigger and differently. They consider and make big changes that prepare their organization for future success.
- Maintainers, improvers, and transformers are all critically needed at every organization.
- Without a transformer mindset, any organization will slowly—or maybe quickly—die.

Chapter 10

Get off the X

On April 15, 2013, Zach and his family were in Boston to cheer on his dad, who was running the 117th Boston Marathon. It was a special day, as this is one of the world's most iconic races, and simply qualifying for the race is a huge achievement.

Thousands of spectators line the streets of Boston to cheer on runners, so Zach and his family got to the finish line early to get a good position to see his dad finish. They found a spot on Boylston Street, about 100 yards from the finish line, with a clear view of the runners as they approached the end of the race.

Right around the time his dad was expected to cross the finish line, Zach heard a loud explosion from across the street. Thinking it was a ceremonial cannon to celebrate Patriots Day, a state holiday that honors the start of the American Revolution, Zach didn't recognize the danger. Seconds later, a second explosion went off, and he instantly knew this wasn't a celebration.

Fearing additional explosions, Zach pushed through the metal barricade separating spectators from runners to get his family away from buildings and possible danger. At the time, he didn't know where to go or what was coming next, but the one thing he did know was that they had to move.

They had to "Get off the X."

Over the next several hours, Zach and his family navigated through the streets of Boston until they were able to safely get back to their hotel.

Thankfully, Zach and his family were not injured in the 2013 Boston Marathon bombings, but sadly, three people were killed, and more than 500 others were injured that day.

Our Correct Craft leaders are continually faced with challenges, though thankfully not as severe as this horrible bombing. A key mindset our team embraces is that when faced with challenges, a leader must "Get off the X."

Lessons From a Former CIA Agent

In her book, *Get off the X: CIA Secrets for Conquering Obstacles and Achieving Your Life's Mission,* former CIA agent Michele Rigby Assad describes the training new agents receive in the CIA Academy. During the "Security and Counter-Ambush" course, they are taught to survive dangerous situations by getting off the "X," also known as the kill zone, as quickly as possible.

Michele has personally been to Correct Craft and spoken to our team a couple of times. We were initially introduced to this idea for the first time when she spoke to us.

Michele says that when faced with a life-or-death situation, people have two choices. The first choice is to run towards the problem and overtake the enemy. This may require fighting using any nearby object as a weapon. The second option, and many times the best option, is to run from the danger to find safe shelter, survive, and fight another day. Agents are trained to quickly decide between the first and second options depending on the situation, but they are taught that the one thing they absolutely cannot do is freeze on the "X."

The freeze response is a deadly mistake that takes practice to overcome. The same is true for business leaders. It is important for people to move outside of their comfort zone to break stagnation and achieve their goals.

Swirling

At Correct Craft, we use the lessons learned from *Get off the X* to keep from swirling. As discussed in Chapter 4, swirling can bog down an organization from reaching its potential and needed results.

It's frustrating and de-energizing to teams, and slows execution of important strategies. Eventually, trust in leadership erodes, and good employees choose to leave an organization.

Sometimes, even the best leaders find themselves in situations where they and their teams are swirling. This is very common when dealing with uncertain risk and the fear of making the wrong decision. Over the years, our Correct Craft team has completed numerous acquisitions, and while they are all vastly different, it's certain that a surprise will pop up during the due diligence process. Many times, these surprises come down to who will accept responsibility for a future risk, so our team works closely with the seller to find an equitable solution. It's very common for these uncertain risks to cause teams to swirl.

A few years ago, our team was going through due diligence on an acquisition, and everything seemed to be going very smoothly. The business fit perfectly in the Correct Craft family, and the seller was very happy that the new owners of their family business were going to honor their legacy and invest in the team. As we were getting to the end of due diligence and nearer to the closing date, an unexpected obstacle came up related to a previous warranty concern. The team began discussing the potential problem, and as the discussions went on, the potential outcomes seemed more catastrophic. Noticing this could lead the team to swirl, Zach decided to quantify a worst-case scenario and a best-case scenario for possible outcomes, knowing that getting out of the abstract and into concrete information would help the team make a decision. Through quantifying the risk, the team was able to "get off the X" and find a workable solution. Interestingly, once quantified, the team realized the problem wasn't that big. The company is now a wonderful member of the Correct Craft family.

Getting out of the abstract to the concrete helped the Correct Craft team stop swirling and get off the X.

Get Out of Your Comfort Zone

If you dread speaking in front of groups, you are not alone. Prominent U.S. research firm R.H. Bruskin Associates published a landmark research study in 1973 that found people actually fear public speaking more than death. This is as true today as it was then. This fear can result in sweaty and shaky hands, a racing heart, and a flustered mind. When on stage, the overwhelming terror of speaking publicly can cause people to freeze, leaving them paralyzed and staring at the audience.

Thankfully, these symptoms can sometimes be managed through diligent preparation and controlled breathing exercises. Although those methods can sometimes help, the best way to overcome the fear of public speaking is to face it or "get off the X." Gradual exposure, like speaking up in meetings and speaking in front of small groups, is a great way to start.

Your comfort zone is the psychological state where you feel safe, familiar, and most comfortable. While comfort zones feel safe, staying in them too long can lead to stagnation. To stretch and grow your comfort zone, you can follow these four steps.

1. Stretch in small steps – Choose challenges that are slightly uncomfortable, but are doable. Growth happens at the edge of uncomfortable, not at extremes.
2. Normalize discomfort – Embrace the truth that when you are uncomfortable, you are growing.
3. Increase the challenges gradually – As something becomes easier, increase the challenge. This can be done by upping the stakes, adding complexity, or adding responsibility.
4. Repeat until the process becomes familiar – Expanding your comfort zone takes practice and patience. Keep at it until it becomes familiar.

Dale Carnegie

In 2014, Zach and a group of colleagues from Correct Craft signed up for an eight-week Dale Carnegie course. This course was based on Carnegie's best-selling book *How to Win Friends and Influence People* and was designed to help Zach and his co-workers improve their public speaking skills. While excited to take the class, Zach knew the purpose of the class was to stretch him outside his comfort zone.

The class instructor, Ken, would have Zach and his group do outlandish improv skits in front of the class, with the exercises getting wilder each week. Zach initially dreaded each session, but as the weeks went by, his attitude began to shift. What once felt intimidating became something he genuinely looked forward to. The more Zach stretched himself, the larger his comfort zone became.

A primary reason people get stuck is fear. Their anxieties become crippling and can cause stagnation in relationships, careers, and life. The best leaders are willing to "get off the X' and step out of their comfort zone, embrace the discomfort, and move forward.

Make a Power Move

When hesitation, fear, or comfort would otherwise keep you stuck on the "X," sometimes it's best to make a power move. A power move is a decisive, forward action that helps people get unstuck. A power move is not about aggression or dominance, but instead focuses on a deliberate action that reclaims control and momentum in the face of uncertainty.

The logic of a power move focuses on these five things.

1. Action over paralysis – this breaks the freeze response.
2. Agency over circumstances – shift from being a victim to ownership.
3. Forward motion – momentum drives progress.
4. Small yet decisive – a power move does not need to be dramatic.

5. Intentional instead of impulsive – a power move is purpose-driven and aligns with values and mission.

In April of 2020, the world was in a frenzy as the COVID pandemic was in its early stages. With limited understanding of where the virus originated or how to stop its spread, people watched friends, coworkers, and family members fall seriously ill—and in some cases, lose their lives.

The leaders at Correct Craft had to balance keeping their teams safe while also trying to provide them jobs to support the families who depended on them. Countless meetings were held to determine the best path forward and how to keep people safe. Temperature checks were conducted as employees entered the workplace to prevent a contagious person from entering. Masks were issued, and the production lines were spaced in a way to maximize social distancing.

Unfortunately, even with those drastic measures, it became evident to us that continuing production posed too great a risk. We made the decision to temporarily shut down operations in the best interest of the team and the company.

In the face of uncertainty, fear, and high emotions, this was a power move. The best leaders are willing to make a power move to "get off the X."

Be an Agent of Influence

When people are swirling, it takes an agent of influence to move first, break the inertia, and make a decision. What's amazing is that when one person makes the first move, it's common for others to follow.

In meetings at Correct Craft, if it becomes evident the team is swirling on a topic, you will often hear someone speak up and say, "Let's stop swirling on this." That one simple phrase by an agent of influence is all it takes for the team to recognize and make the proper adjustments to move forward.

The best leaders model the behavior they desire from their teams. Acting decisively when others hesitate will encourage members of their teams to follow suit.

As leaders, we understand that at times we will be put in tough situations that require us to act quickly and decisively. Using lessons from the book, *Get off the X: CIA Secrets for Conquering Obstacles and Achieving Your Life's Mission,* we know that we can either run towards the threat or run away from the threat, but we must certainly not stay on the "X."

In the next chapter, we will learn some additional ways to act decisively and with authority.

Chapter 10 Summary

- You can run to a problem or from a problem, but you can't stay on the "X."
- "Swirling" is an example of being stuck on the "X."
- To expand your comfort zone, you must get out of your comfort zone.
- Growth happens at the edges of comfort, not at the extremes.
- A primary reason people get stuck is fear.
- To get unstuck, make a decisive power move.
- Acting decisively when others hesitate will encourage members of the team to follow.
- The best leaders know to "get off the X."

Be a Fighter Pilot

A fighter pilot is someone who acts with urgency and purpose and will do whatever it takes to accomplish the mission. They prioritize results over comfort, action over debate, and the mission over personal role, title, or recognition.

In March of 2020, right at the beginning of the COVID pandemic, the supply chain team at Nautique received a letter from a vendor that raised an alarm. One of their most critical vendors, the company that supplied all the foam for Nautique's seats and cushions, was going out of business. The shutdown would begin affecting production in a matter of days.

This was a serious problem. Finding a new foam vendor and getting that vendor set up to start producing parts takes time, and the Nautique team didn't have time. They had to act quickly before running out of foam, causing production to halt, which is about the worst thing that can happen in a boat plant.

The Nautique team quickly rallied to find a solution. Team members from product development, model integration, and production formed a "foam team" to build these foam pieces themselves. They went to local hardware stores and purchased tools, and they hand-made jigs and fixtures for the foam configurations needed. A make-shift assembly line was formed in the parking lot, where the team rapidly worked to build the needed parts to keep production running.

We didn't miss a day of boat production. The Nautique team were fighter pilots. After the crisis subsided, we invested in equipment, space, and a dedicated team to move this out of the parking lot and into Nautique's production system.

The COVID pandemic provided a crash course in crisis management. Challenges were everywhere, but the best leaders and teams assumed the mindset of a "fighter pilot."

When faced with a sudden threat to their operations, the Nautique team embraced the mindset of a fighter pilot and acted swiftly.

Making it to tomorrow preserves options. Once you're out of the immediate crisis, you can adapt, learn, and take advantage of future opportunities. Today, the Nautique team is better for the challenge they faced in 2020.

Commercial Pilot Mode

Commercial flying is one of the world's safest forms of transportation, far safer than cars or buses per distance traveled. In fact, statistics show there is only one fatal accident per 2.5 to 5 million flights. Bill and Zach travel often, and they are very comfortable with the training and skills of the commercial pilots in charge of getting them to their destination safely.

Many leaders resemble commercial pilots. Under normal circumstances, they will safely get the organization where it needs to go, and everyone will be happy. They fly the same routes day in and day out, have checklists to ensure consistency, and are reliable.

However, we don't always operate under normal circumstances. Sometimes, we are in crisis or seemingly at war. In those cases, an organization needs fighter pilots who operate with a totally different mindset. Repeatedly, we have seen great commercial pilot leaders fail to turn on the fighter pilot mentality when needed, costing them and their organizations dearly.

Commercial Pilot in a Fighter Pilot Role

A few years ago, we hired someone at Correct Craft to help all our companies with lean manufacturing. We recognized that by focusing on lean principles, we could increase quality, consistency, and safety in our processes and products. The person we hired—let's call him John—had a lot of experience in big organizations and was well-versed in lean system philosophies.

Unfortunately, when problems came up, John didn't bring solutions. While he was focused on the theory of lean systems, John lacked the urgency and problem-solving skills to help the organization in the moments they most needed. John was a great commercial pilot, but he couldn't make the leap to fighter pilot when needed. He actually said when we let him go that "Correct Craft is looking for a fighter pilot, and that isn't me."

Mission Focus

Fighter pilots understand the mission and fully commit to it. As conditions change, as they inevitably do, people with a fighter pilot mindset don't panic or lower standards. They adapt quickly and decisively to push through and will step up, take ownership, and work assertively, even under extreme pressure.

The most important job for a leader in a crisis is to create clarity around the mission and objectives. When clarity is missing, organizations begin to swirl. People chase symptoms instead of causes, debate distractions, and mistake activity for progress. Confusion spreads quickly, and momentum is lost.

Leaders with a fighter pilot mindset counter this by galvanizing the team towards a clearly stated goal. They continually reinforce what matters most and align decisions, resources, and communication toward that objective. They focus the organization on solutions that move the team closer to the mission, rather than allowing energy to be consumed by side issues or internal noise.

Red Herrings

In a crisis, one of the most common mistakes leaders make is getting captured by red herrings. A red herring is irrelevant or misleading information that diverts attention away from the core problem. Red herrings are especially dangerous because they waste time and energy in an already stressful situation. In high-stakes environments, identifying and ignoring red herrings is critical.

The ability to stay focused on what truly matters often determines whether you succeed or even survive tomorrow. All leaders will face a crisis at some point during their career, and when that happens, the best leaders become fighter pilots.

Leave Your Ego at the Door

In fighter pilot mode, no task is beneath anyone. The mission matters more than titles, job descriptions, or personal recognition. Ego must be left at the door.

Zach and Bill have both heard people say something along the lines of "if you give me that promotion I have been wanting, or give me a raise, then I will do more." When we hear that, a warning flag immediately goes up.

Crisis situations are the times when the best leaders stand out from the crowd. They view these as opportunities to learn and will do whatever is necessary to help the company. As discussed in Chapter 1, instead of focusing on titles, money, or rewards, they focus on impact.

Zach saw this dynamic a few years ago. An unplanned production delay came up at one of our Correct Craft companies that threatened to negatively impact an important customer. The team had recently worked hard to win the business, and the delay was going to put the relationship at risk.

In the middle of the situation, a team member, who Zach respected and was very important to the team, called Zach and said, "If you give me a promotion, I will go rally a group and get these orders out on time." Zach immediately recognized this was a problem. The request shifted the focus from the mission to individual gain at the very moment the team needed him most. Zach found another solution to meet the customer's expectations. That person did not fit us. We get things done because we choose impact; we want to help people, not just look for rewards.

People with a fighter pilot mindset leave their ego at the door and put the team results over individual recognition. As discussed in Chapter 1, when people focus on impact, the title, money, and rewards will take care of themselves.

Calm is Contagious

In high-stress situations, a fighter pilot's calm demeanor benefits everyone else flying with them. They are trained to remain calm so they can process incoming information quickly and with clarity.

The same is true in business. Leaders set the emotional tone. When leaders remain steady under pressure, teams perform better.

Teams take cues, often subconsciously, from how leaders speak, act, and react. When leaders become visibly anxious, reactive, or erratic, that behavior spreads quickly, eroding trust and performance.

Alternatively, when leaders remain calm under pressure, they create space for clarity and execution. Calm leaders listen better, think more clearly, and make higher-quality decisions. More importantly, they give their teams confidence that challenges are manageable and that the mission is still achievable.

Calm does not mean passive. Fighter pilots can be calm and decisive at the same time. The same is true for leaders. The best leaders have the ability to project steadiness while acting with urgency. In turbulent moments, calm becomes contagious, allowing teams to perform at their best.

Debriefs Matter

A core part of a fighter pilot's training is a debrief after every mission. In these debriefs, pilots and essential support staff go through flight information, mission details, and results to turn every mission into a learning experience. An important aspect of these debriefs is that they are often peer-led and rank agnostic. This allows for honest feedback where rank is set aside to foster open and effective communication.

The same principle applies to leadership and business, especially after a crisis. Too often, once the crisis is over, teams rush back to normal operations without taking the necessary time to reflect on the lessons learned. Opportunities for learning are missed, leaving the company vulnerable to making the same mistakes when the next crisis inevitably comes.

In a debrief, it is important for the leader to focus on foundational lessons, and not only on the specifics of the mission. This is because the likelihood of that specific event happening again is low, while the likelihood of another unforeseen crisis is high.

A PEG Example

A few years ago, the Pleasurecraft Engine Group team had a situation where a large batch of engine blocks came with a faulty component. This faulty component affected a lot of engine blocks in stock and was going to take a significant amount of time and energy to fix. Mark McKinney, then President of Pleasurecraft Engine Group, acted quickly to find a solution before the problem affected his customers. After solving the problem and during the debrief, the Pleasurecraft Engine Group team focused on learning lessons that would apply to any defect, not only to the one they had just faced.

Leaders with a fighter pilot mindset insist on debriefs. They create an environment where learning is essential and protect against a fear-based "gotcha" culture. When they do this, their company and their teams come out far better for doing so.

As Winston Churchill is credited with saying, "Never waste a good crisis."

Fighter Pilot to Commercial Pilot

Operating in fighter pilot mode is taxing on the leader, the team, and the organization. Prolonged periods of high stress and intensity can be detrimental to team culture, causing frustration and turnover on the team.

The best leaders know how to switch modes from fighter pilot in crisis to commercial pilot in stability. Sometimes the mistake isn't becoming a fighter pilot; it's staying one too long. Below are ways people can shift from fighter pilot mode back to commercial pilot.

- **Replace heroics with systems:** In fighter pilot mode, people improvise and stretch to survive. In commercial pilot mode, leaders capture what worked and turn it into repeatable systems.
- **Intentionally slow the decision tempo:** Crisis demands speed; stability demands quality. Switch from intuition-driven decisions to data-driven decisions.
- **Move from command to empower:** Fighter pilot mode often centralizes authority, commercial pilot mode pushes decisions back to the teams.
- **Normalize planning again:** In a crisis, plans are short-term and tactical. In commercial mode, leaders look into the future again.

Just as important as it is for leaders to have a fighter pilot mentality, the best leaders are also able to get their teams out of crisis mode quickly and shift back to being commercial pilots. This frees up space to ensure the organization is prepared to handle another potential crisis. This is what happened at Nautique with the foam team. After getting through the initial challenges, the Nautique team was able to shift from being fighter pilots in a parking lot assembly line to building a sustainable process that now helps the company through vertical integration.

Conclusion

Zach and Bill's leadership style is to mutually agree with our team on goals, and then let them work toward achieving them. We don't think anyone would accuse us of being micromanagers. However, there are times when a leader must step in, manage assertively, and make tough calls as a fighter pilot would. Maybe the best example of this is during an economic or market downturn, when the leader must protect the organization. Leaders who can endure when times get hard have a fighter pilot mindset.

Next, in chapter 12, we will discuss the importance of creativity.

Chapter 11 Summary

- Leaders who can endure when times get hard have a fighter pilot mindset.
- Fighter pilots fully commit to the mission and do everything they can to accomplish it.
- The most important job for a leader in a crisis is to create clarity around the mission and objectives.
- When in crisis, a leader must be willing to work outside their job description.
- Fighter pilots are calm and decisive at the same time.
- As soon as possible, good leaders focus on retuning from fighter pilot to commercial pilot.

Creativity Over Capital

One summer, Bill's family enjoyed a wonderful cruise through the Caribbean aboard *Mariner of the Seas,* a Royal Caribbean ship. Visits to Haiti, Jamaica, and the Bahamas were interspersed with relaxing days at sea. All his family members love cruising, so it was a great time.

On one of the days at sea, they had a behind-the-scenes tour of the ship's operations. To say its processes are impressive is a significant understatement. The ship is a well-oiled machine. They saw how the crew managed on-board inventory, food service, mechanical matters, laundry, crew housing, crew off time, and more. Everything was done with a high degree of excellence, which was consistent with the experience they had as guests.

Cruise-Ship Good

And the most amazing part? They manage everything with very little space. Sure, the cruise ship is big, especially compared with the boats we build at Correct Craft, but most of its space is devoted to living areas and amenities for the thousands of guests and crew. The actual space for the operations of a floating city is small.

Mariner of the Seas' operations must be efficient; there is no choice. Limited room and an inability to restock at sea require optimal use of space. The tour reminded Bill of time spent studying Lean Six Sigma—a process improvement methodology—when he first began fully understanding how space can be the enemy. A cruise ship's limited space forces it to be efficient, and that is a good thing. Bill was so impressed with the boat's operations that he had to share the experience with our Correct Craft team. The experience has led us to begin using a new term that helps our team visualize how we want to be: "Cruise-Ship Good."

Leaders who are forced to manage through space constraints likely operate more efficiently. We have seen this firsthand throughout the companies they have led for years. This is the basis for the mindset "Creativity over Capital."

Creativity Drives Innovation

Constraints are often viewed as obstacles to overcome, but in reality, they are powerful catalysts for innovation. When leaders face limits, whether in space, capital, time, or talent, they are forced to think differently. Constraints force leaders to use their creativity to find better answers, and that is good.

Instead of asking, "How do we execute this idea?" leaders must ask, "Is this the right idea at all?" Creating clarity around the real problem to be solved allows teams to break out of the "It's always been done this way" thinking and explore new alternatives. Many breakthroughs come not from doing things faster or cheaper, but by using creativity to do things differently.

Southwest Airlines

This is something startup airline Southwest did in 1972 when facing serious financial strain. At the time, Southwest had just sold one of its four Boeing 737s to raise cash but still needed to maintain service to its core routes. To compete, Southwest's Vice President of Ground Operations, Bill Franklin, challenged his team to use their creativity to turn each aircraft around at the gate in just ten minutes. This was far faster than industry norms at the time.

The Southwest team was able to do this by standardizing to one aircraft type, eliminating unnecessary cabin services, using open seating to speed up the boarding process, and cross-training employees (gate agents also helped with cabin cleaning). By creatively rethinking the entire process, Southwest was able to improve aircraft utilization and record its first profit the following year.

Think Like an Outsider

Often, disruption in an industry happens through an outsider. That person isn't blinded by the traditional way of thinking and can solve problems in totally different ways. When looking at challenges, we encourage you to think like an outsider. The best leaders are able to use constraints as a catalyst for innovation. Not getting caught in the old ways of thinking is a competitive advantage.

The Problem With More

In unconstrained environments, the default response to a problem is often to use capital and add—more people, more equipment, more facilities. However, the unintended consequences of those decisions can wipe away any expected benefits and the capital has been spent.

An example of this is adding people capital. In boat manufacturing, onboarding new employees is a long process, taking anywhere from several months to a year before the new employee is fully trained, costing a lot of capital. During that time, the most experienced team members step into mentor roles, slowing their pace to teach the standards and skills required to do the job. This can add to frustration within the team and can have negative impacts on quality during training times.

Besides using various forms of capital, adding headcount also takes a long time to accomplish, slowing progress while waiting to find the right employees. This delay can paralyze an organization, even causing it to miss out on the opportunity it is chasing.

COVID Impact

The COVID pandemic was horrible in many ways, but in one way, it was actually a blessing for the boating business. While people were social distancing, not traveling, and avoiding large gatherings, a great activity for families to enjoy was boating. We saw record boat sales, leaving our dealers with little inventory and begging for more boats.

At the same time, finding employees to build the boats was extremely challenging. Unemployment was near zero, making competition high and driving wages up quickly. This labor constraint became a primary bottleneck to increasing production to meet the unexpected demand of the market. Unfortunately, by the time many companies were staffed and ready to increase production, the demand was already falling. The delay caused them to miss out on an opportunity and left them overstaffed right when the market pulled back.

Before using capital to add more employees, equipment, or space, the best leaders ensure the current resources are being fully maximized. Simply adding resources to a poorly planned process only magnifies the inefficiencies that exist. We have visited hundreds of manufacturing facilities around the world, and we have seen this repeatedly. More equipment and space do not always generate better results.

A Danger of Success

During a recent expansion project at one of the Correct Craft companies, rising construction costs began pushing the budget beyond plan. The team had to make tough choices, cutting some of the "wish list" items to stay on track.

During the discussion, a team leader was really pushing for a larger breakroom that was much grander than the original plan. He argued, if we really cared about employees, we should invest in this space—and Correct Craft had the capital to make it happen.

Bill responded by reframing the conversation. He reminded the team that the best way to care for employees is by ensuring the company remains strong and sustainable for the long haul. We want to make smart financial decisions with our capital so that Correct Craft is around to provide jobs to employees for as long as they would like. Poor financial choices, even with the best intentions, ultimately do the opposite.

The Risk of Having Capital

Having access to resources or capital can create the temptation to spend freely. Correct Craft has been successful, and because of that success, it has the resources to invest where it is smart to do so. It's essential for leaders to resist the trap of not protecting capital and make disciplined, strategic decisions that ensure the organization remains strong, sustainable, and capable of providing lasting value for employees and the business. Without this discipline, even successful companies risk undermining the people they aim to support.

Eliminate Lazy Solutions

Constraints also force leaders to use creativity to eliminate lazy solutions. When resources are limited, there is no room for half-measures. Leaders and teams must address inefficiencies head-on, rather than masking them with more staff, bigger budgets, or expanded facilities. It is important to resist the "lift and shift" mentality of moving inefficient processes into larger spaces, which just makes the problem worse.

In manufacturing, this might mean redesigning a workstation to reduce motion waste, retraining employees to follow a standardized process, or rearranging inventory for maximum efficiency. In service or administrative functions, it could involve automating repetitive tasks or simplifying workflows. In every case, the goal is to maximize results from the resources already available.

A Framework for Investment Decisions

Capital allocation is one of the most important responsibilities of a CEO. Poor investments can be costly and have lasting consequences. To guide decision-making, leaders should ask four essential questions before approving any significant capital investment:

1. **What problem are we trying to solve?**
    - Clarify the underlying issue to avoid spending money on symptoms rather than the root cause.

2. **What would we do if capital were not available?**
    - Forcing teams to think creatively without relying on additional funds often uncovers better, simpler solutions.

3. **Have we explored all options?**
    - Innovation often comes from rethinking existing processes, cross-training staff, or reallocating resources before spending money.

4. **Does this decision strengthen the company long-term?**
    - Every investment should increase sustainability, not just provide short-term gratification.

Answering these questions ensures that capital is deployed thoughtfully, aligned with strategy, and supportive of long-term innovation.

Conclusion

Constraints drive creativity and innovation. They force teams to use all currently available space and resources to their fullest potential to maximize results. The best leaders operate as if constraints are present, even when capital is abundant, to maximize efficiencies, eliminate waste, and produce better outcomes.

Before investing in big, capital-intensive projects, we encourage you to have the mindset of creativity over capital. The leaders who do this well achieve greater long-term and sustainable results.

In our next chapter, we will explore how to identify and tackle the most important items, what we call juggling monkeys.

Chapter 12 Summary

- Before investing in capital, the best leaders ensure their current resources are fully maximized.
- Constraints are often catalysts for innovation.
- "More" does not always drive better results.
- Don't "lift and shift" a bad process into a bigger footprint.
- The best leaders operate as if constraints are present, even if capital is abundant.

Juggling Monkeys

Have you ever taught a monkey to juggle?

No? You're not alone; most leaders haven't. And oddly enough, that might be why many leaders, and their teams, have trouble completing projects, even after thinking the project was on track.

Over the years that has happened to us. We have been told that a project was on track, only to learn later that it missed its deadline. Or it quietly died altogether. How does this happen? Why would a conscientious and high-integrity leader tell us their team was nearly done with a project when they weren't? More often than not, they actually thought they were on track.

So, what went wrong?

The answer is simple – and sneaky. The team failed to account for the juggling monkey.

At Correct Craft, we've learned to identify these monkeys early and teach them to juggle first. Doing so has become a critical discipline for ensuring projects are completed on time, and commitments are kept.

Understanding the Juggling Monkey

The concept of "Juggling Monkey" is often attributed to Astro Teller, a highly intelligent person who leads many of Google's most ambitious initiatives, such as self-driving cars and other complex projects. The idea is elegant and powerful. We'll try to describe it below.

Imagine you come up with a brilliant business idea - one that you are certain will be a money-maker. You are going to place a monkey on a pedestal in a local park and charge people to watch the monkey juggle. To get started, you identify twelve steps that must be completed to begin your new business.

- Find the right park
- Secure permits
- Buy materials for the pedestal
- Acquire a monkey
- And so on

You complete eleven of the twelve steps, so it's safe to conclude you're over 90% done, right?

Maybe, but what if the remaining step is teaching the monkey to juggle?

That one step – the hardest, most uncertain, and most time consuming – determines whether the entire project succeeds or fails. And until it's done, progress elsewhere doesn't really matter.

That step is what we call the juggling monkey.

A False Sense of Progress

Most teams naturally knock out the easiest steps first. It feels productive. Boxes get checked. Status reports look good. Momentum feels real.

But when the most critical task—teaching the monkey to juggle—is left until the end, teams develop a dangerous false sense of progress. Deadlines get missed. Commitments are broken. And sometimes leaders discover, far too late, that the most important step can't be completed at all—meaning all the earlier work was effectively wasted.

We've seen this pattern play out frequently in strategic planning. Strategic plans often span multiple years and include long lists of initiatives. Teams feel successful as they check off task after task. Then the plan period ends, and often the team is content with being "90 percent complete."

But the real question is: Which 10 percent didn't get done?

Too often, those missing steps are the juggling monkeys—the ones that actually determine whether the strategy delivers meaningful results. When they're ignored, teams stay busy and believe they have accomplished a lot, but never reach the outcomes that truly matter.

Focus on the Right Things

That's why, at Correct Craft, every team is required to identify their juggling monkeys when developing strategic plans. We want to focus on the right things.

Not Just for Strategic Planning

The juggling monkey mindset isn't limited to large, multi-year initiatives. It's just as powerful for small projects and even daily work.

Once this concept becomes part of your thinking—and your vocabulary—it changes how teams operate. In our meetings, it's common to hear someone ask, "What's the juggling monkey here?"

That one question often saves months of wasted effort.

Meet Thomas Bates

Over the past two decades, Thomas Bates, who is now Correct Craft's Chief Revenue Officer, has repeatedly stepped into complex, high-pressure situations. One of his first moves in each role is always the same: identify the juggling monkeys.

Several years ago, Bill asked Thomas to take over the Product Development team at one of our companies. The team faced immediate challenges, and Bill trusted Thomas to address them quickly.

Thomas wasted no time. He identified three key juggling monkeys:

1. Innovation Focus & Product Discipline - Product complexity slowed the team down. Thomas limited each new model to two or three core innovations and deliberately staged additional

ideas across the product lifecycle. This protected launch timing, reduced risk, and sustained long-term sales growth.

2. Strategic Alignment Through Design Charters - The design charter process, which identifies what work is to be done, lacked discipline. Thomas tightened it to ensure executive leadership, corporate strategy, and product priorities were aligned from the start. This eliminated scope creep, clarified decision boundaries, reduced rework, and enabled faster, higher-quality decisions without constant executive escalation.

3. Parallel Design & Engineering Execution - Sequential handoffs between design and engineering were creating friction and late-stage redesigns. Thomas introduced parallel collaboration to align teams earlier. The result: less rework, shorter development cycles, and higher product quality.

Many leaders would have spent months swirling in a new role without ever reaching the root causes. Thomas didn't. With a juggling monkey mindset, he quickly identified the real problems and acted.

This is another clear example of the principle we introduced in Chapter 4: Results > Activity.

Personal Application

Identifying your juggling monkeys—and ensuring they are addressed—dramatically increases your ability to get things done. This mindset has helped our teams achieve big goals, and it has helped each of us personally as well.

By now, it should be clear that we believe mindset is essential for success, both professionally and personally. This book outlines fifteen mindsets that have shaped our journey.

Any one of these fifteen mindsets could be your personal juggling monkey—the one thing holding you back from the next level of impact.

Do you need to become a learner?

Choose impact?

Get off the X?

Embrace one of the other mindsets in this book?

Which one, if mastered, would change everything?

Once you identify your personal juggling monkey and begin working on it intentionally, both your professional and personal life will improve. And not in a small way – in a huge way!

A Few Other Helpful Mindsets

While we have identified the key mindsets that have helped our Correct Craft team achieve and have an impact, your personal juggling monkey might be different. Below are a few additional ideas worth considering:

- **Expect a lot of yourself** - Most people only achieve a small bit of their potential. Not because they cannot do more, but because they don't expect more of themselves. Many are unwilling to push themselves enough to get close to their true potential. A key to personal success is thinking big and then taking the necessary actions to achieve your big goals. If coming home each evening to watch TV or spending the weekend on a couch sounds appealing, that's a fine choice, but don't expect to accomplish anything big. Set huge goals and expect yourself to do whatever is necessary to achieve them.
- **See opportunity in everything** - Challenges are unavoidable. Most people see them as obstacles and retreat. Others— often guided by stoic thinking—see them as opportunities others will avoid. As our team often says, "The obstacle is the way." Successful people see challenges as an opportunity to achieve something others cannot.
- **Think positive** - Martin Seligman, one of the world's leading researchers on optimism and a professor at the University of Pennsylvania, has clearly documented the benefits of thinking

optimistically. Much of his work can be read in his excellent and classic book, *Learned Optimism*. Sometimes, people downplay a positive mindset, arguing that it ignores reality, but that's not true. Someone with a positive mindset sees things as they are. Pessimists—or as they often call themselves, realists—often see things as worse than they are, because they are looking through a lens colored by fear or insecurity.

Understanding and embracing the importance of juggling monkeys can be career- and life-changing. It helps you focus on what's important, whether it is a project or your personal career.

In the next chapter we will discuss the importance of thinking big.

Chapter 13 Summary

- Identifying your juggling monkeys is critical to the success of any project.
- Don't save the most important—and often most difficult—step for the end of a project.
- If you haven't identified the juggling monkeys, you likely have a false sense of progress.
- The Juggling Monkey mindset is as powerful when applied personally as it is professionally.

Visualization (10X Thinking/Backcasting)

We have mentioned a few times how in 2009, our company generated $39 million in annual revenue. By 2023, that number had grown to more than $1 billion. That kind of growth doesn't happen by accident. Many factors contributed to our success, but one in particular played a critical role: visualization—the ability to clearly see, believe in, and commit to a successful future before it becomes reality.

Visualization is not wishful thinking. It is a disciplined way of imagining what can be, and then aligning people, strategy, and action to make it happen.

Seeing it Before it Happens

Bill's first exposure to visualization happened as a college student while reading about the success of professional golfer, Jack Nicklaus. Bill's dad was a big Nicklaus fan, and Bill even crossed paths with Jack from time to time at local ball fields, where Bill played sports in the same leagues as Nicklaus's sons.

So, when reading a book about Nicklaus, arguably golf's greatest player, it was intriguing to learn that Nicklaus attributed a big part of his success to visualization. Nicklaus spoke about vivid mental imagery that was important to his game and accomplishments. The swing, the ball flight, and exactly where the ball would land would be visualized by Nicklaus before each shot.

Nicklaus' visualization set the stage for innumerable athletes who followed him. Simone Biles, Usain Bolt, Tom Brady, Michael Jordan,

Cristiano Renaldo, Lindsey Vonn, Serena Williams, and Tiger Woods are just a few of the athletes who have spoken openly about the importance of visualization as an important part of their mental preparation.

But visualization is not limited to athletics.

Successful actor Jim Carrey is well known for writing a check to himself for $10 million when he was getting started; he labeled it "for acting services." He was visualizing receipt of that check. Others known for practicing visualization include Oprah Winfrey, Elon Musk, and Richard Branson. Visualization can help anyone achieve their goals, regardless of what they are working to accomplish.

Visualization also delivers benefits that go well beyond achievement or performance. There are reports of visualization helping with stress reduction, learning and memory issues, and overall health and healing.

We know visualization has helped us at Correct Craft.

What the Research Shows

The preceding may seem like a lot of anecdotal evidence, but visualization has been well-researched.

- Studies published in both the *Journal of Sports Sciences* and the *Journal of Experimental Psychology* have validated that visualization can improve sports performance.
- Studies published in the *Journal of Behavioral Medicine* and the *Journal of Consulting and Clinical Psychology* have shown that visualization provides health benefits.
- The American Psychological Association acknowledges it can help with stress reduction.
- Research published in the *European Journal of Social Psychology* demonstrated that visualization helps people achieve goals, whatever those goals are.

In short, visualization works.

Visualization at Correct Craft

So, how did visualization help our company grow more than 25X times over fifteen years?

In short, it is an important part of our strategic planning process, which includes big goals, and makes up half of our secret sauce, the other half being culture.

10X Thinking

A core element of our visualization process at Correct Craft is called 10X thinking. Instead of asking how we can get 10 or 20 percent better, we ask how we can get 10X better?

10X thinking significantly expands the possibilities of what can be done. It may seem odd but often thinking about how to do something better by 10X is easier to consider than a 2X improvement. This is because when most people think of 2X improvement, they think "work harder." However, people know that 10X growth or improvement requires more than just trying harder; it requires something different – a new approach, a new model, or an entirely new way of thinking.

Even though it is counterintuitive, 10X thinking often feels easier. In fact, it can be liberating, opening the door for creativity, innovation, and breakthrough ideas. And that is the first step to developing a plan for significant growth or improvement.

We also use visualization to create Big Hairy Audacious Goals (BHAGs). Jim Collins developed the idea of a BHAG in his book *Built to Last: Successful Habits of Visionary Companies*. The technique is used to imagine and chase a goal that might seem unreachable. We discuss and create BHAG's with a 10X mindset.

Backcasting: Starting at the Finish Line

Visualization becomes even more powerful when combined with backcasting.

Backcasting flips traditional planning on its head. And it is a very effective tool that helps people unlock their thinking about the future. We use it, in conjunction with 10X thinking, at all our Correct Craft companies when kicking off a new strategic plan.

Basically, backcasting works by creating an exciting and optimistic future and telling the team that *the bright future has already been achieved*. We usually do this by creating a fictional newspaper article dated five years in the future, with a headline that says something like,

> "Company tripled its sales with all-time high customer
> and employee satisfaction."

Using the fictional newspaper article to present the goal as already achieved helps the team think in terms of how they did it versus how they will do it. It is much easier for a group to think about and describe how they have already accomplished something even if it is fictional than to think of how to achieve something in the future.

It may seem unconventional, but we have seen backcasting successfully used many times. It's a powerful mind hack that quickly unlocks thinking.

How It All Comes Together

10X thinking and backcasting are part of Correct Craft's visualization process, which is the foundation of our strategic planning.

After creating clarity on where we want to go, we start by developing a detailed situation analysis with input from primarily outside sources. Once we have a clear picture of our current situation, the leadership team of the company working on the new strategic plan creates an overall BHAG for their company.

But visualization does not stop there.

Next, we identify the company's primary functions; usually there are about twelve—i.e., product development, production, supply chain, sales, marketing, finance, human resources, etc. The leader of each of these functional areas develops another BHAG specifically for their area of responsibility. The plan is set up so that if each functional team achieves its BHAG, the overall company BHAG is reached.

While this may seem complex, it is actually very simple. The best part is that having our leaders visualize what their team can do over the next strategic planning period helps them improve their results. Combining backcasting and BHAGs helps our team picture what we can accomplish, and then the team goes out and does it.

Visualization has helped our team achieve 25X growth. You may not, or you may, reach that level of growth, but we guarantee you will do better using visualization than you would without it. We have seen it work repeatedly, helping people and organizations achieve great results.

Centurion and Supreme Boats

After acquiring the Centurion and Supreme brands more than a decade ago, we immediately applied the principles shared in this chapter. And frankly, it scared some people. The team was not used to thinking in these terms, and a couple of key executives resigned because of it.

We were sorry to see them go, but we also wanted people on board who would embrace the mindsets we were trying to establish.

The results speak for themselves. Centurion and Supreme have enjoyed significant growth during the last decade as part of Correct Craft. Revenue and profit have both increased by multiples. Maybe the most impressive part? In a very competitive market, Centurion and Supreme have more than doubled their market share.

The success we have had at Centurion and Supreme has fueled a significant positive impact. We have funded a considerable number of community service projects in the Merced, California area. We have also paid bonuses to every single employee at the company, collectively millions of dollars, which have made the lives of our team and families better. Most of that bonus money was spent by our employees in the Merced community, further extending our positive impact on the area.

We have seen repeatedly the significant positive impact of visualization. It's not just Centurion and Supreme; it's across all our Correct Craft companies.

A Personal Example

Visualization is not just for organizations – it works for individuals too.

Recently, a friend of Bill's was preparing to speak at an important business leader's meeting, and she was very nervous. Bill wanted to be helpful and told her to visualize walking up on the stage and giving the best speech of her life, to imagine exactly how her amazing speech would go, and visualize the crowd loving it.

She did exactly that, and it helped a lot.

Almost immediately after her presentation, Bill received a text from the event organizer, a mutual friend, saying it was the best speech ever given to this group. Visualization helped her and can help us be successful.

A Challenge to You

Our challenge for anyone reading this book is to visualize where you and your organization will be in five and ten years, and to think big, really big.

We have heard it said that people tend to overestimate what they can accomplish in one year and underestimate what they can achieve in five years. You can accomplish way more than you think; the first step is visualization. Don't waste any more time; visualize a great future for you and your organization.

Start today.

Visualization matters, but it only becomes reality through action, which is why the next chapter, *Be a River, Not a Reservoir*, focuses on turning knowledge and leadership into forward-moving momentum.

Chapter 14 Summary

- A lot of successful people in a variety of fields attribute their success to visualization.
- Visualization is an important tool for organizations, too.
- 10X thinking is an important mindset that makes visualization powerful.
- Backcasting is a tool that unlocks thinking related to visualization and 10X thinking.
- Visualization, combined with a 10x thinking mindset and backcasting, will help individuals and organizations achieve big things.

Be a River, not a Reservoir

Mark McKinney, President of Liberty Technologies, is one of the most knowledgeable people in the world when it comes to designing and engineering inboard marine engines. As described in Chapter 9, Mark is a true transformer. He has spent decades in the industry taking engine blocks and marinizing them for use in many of today's inboard towboats. His experience is deep, hard-earned, and extraordinarily valuable.

Mark's expertise didn't come from textbooks alone. It came from years of problem-solving, redesigns, and hard decisions. He has seen what works, what doesn't, and just as importantly, why. That kind of knowledge is rare, and organizations that rely on it without intention put themselves at risk.

Because we value Mark so highly, we don't expect him to work forever. In fact, honoring great leaders means planning well before they leave. A few years ago, Zach and Bill sat down with Mark to talk about succession—not as a retirement conversation, but as a stewardship conversation. We knew that because Mark had been at the center of so many critical projects, replacing him wouldn't involve just a single person or a quick transition. It would require multiple people, time, discipline, and a deliberate transfer of knowledge.

This is where the idea of "being a river, not a reservoir" became central.

We asked Mark to be a river. That meant involving his team deeply in projects instead of solving every problem himself. It meant slowing down at times to teach, explain, and document, even when it would have been faster for him to simply handle it personally. Mark embraced the river mindset and has invested heavily in his team to leave Liberty Technologies in a better position when he eventually retires.

The strongest leaders are rivers, not reservoirs, and share information throughout the organization.

Why the Secrets?

Many leaders rationalize being a reservoir by convincing themselves that the information they have is confidential and must be protected. Interestingly, we find this rarely to be true. In most cases, the information is not as secret as some people may think.

Zach once worked with a leader, we will call him Ed, who had a habit of holding information close. Ed was a reservoir. He believed that limiting what his team knew helped him stay in control and reduce risk. In reality, doing so had the opposite effect.

Since key information wasn't shared, Ed's team was constantly reacting instead of anticipating. Priorities were unclear, decisions were delayed, and work often had to be redone once new information surfaced. The lack of transparency drained energy from the team, created frustration, and ultimately led to high turnover and underperformance.

During a conversation with Ed, Zach challenged him to rethink his approach. He encouraged Ed to share more openly about priorities and goals. Over time, by changing his mindset and becoming a river, Ed was able to greatly change the culture and performance of his team for the better. This one simple change had a transformative effect on Ed's team.

Industry trends, performance metrics, strategic priorities, and even operational challenges are often already visible to employees in some form. Employees see customer behavior, production bottlenecks, quality issues, and market pressures every day. That said, not all information should be shared. There are clear and appropriate boundaries. Employee compensation, individual performance evaluations, legal matters, and trade secrets require discretion. However, these exceptions are far narrower than many leaders assume.

The danger arises when leaders label information as "confidential" simply because it feels uncomfortable to share or because sharing it would require them to be vulnerable. Sometimes, the real leaders become reservoirs not out of necessity, but out of habit.

Need to Know vs. Want to Know

Most leaders share information that their team needs to know, but not as many are good at sharing information that their team wants to know.

As leaders, we do everything we can to make sure our team has the information they need to know. This includes providing clarity around goals, expectations, and progress toward those goals. In addition, the best leaders do everything they can to share information that their teams want to know. These are things that on the surface may not seem necessary, but the team appreciates getting updates on them. This provides energy and has a positive impact on team culture and performance.

Want-to-know information may not seem essential at first glance, but it matters deeply. It includes:

- How the business is performing overall.
- What leaders are worried or excited about.
- Industry trends and market shifts.
- Strategic direction beyond the next quarter.
- Context around decisions that affect people's work.

Sharing this kind of information builds trust. It signals respect. It helps people feel connected to something larger than their individual roles.

We have worked hard to do this at Correct Craft by holding regular and frequent updates with our team. We have quarterly full-team meetings where Bill and Zach give updates on the boating market, our performance, and other important events.

Bill also asks each person to come to the meeting with a question. This simple practice opens dialogue and allows what people are really thinking to surface. The questions range widely from business strategy to travel to personal updates and they create space for learning, connection, and transparency.

Leaders who are rivers and not reservoirs actively find ways to engage with their teams and provide them with the information they both need and want to know.

Reservoirs Create Dependency; Rivers Build Capability

A reservoir leader accumulates information, decisions, and expertise. Over time, everything flows to them. They become the bottleneck—not intentionally, but inevitably.

When leaders act as reservoirs:

- Teams wait for answers instead of solving problems.
- Decisions slow down.
- Risk concentrates at the top.
- The organization becomes dependent on individuals instead of systems.

By contrast, river leaders actively push knowledge outward. They develop others to think, decide, and act with context.

River leaders:

- Share information broadly.
- Teach how to reason, not just what to do.
- Build redundancy into capability.
- Strengthen the organization beyond itself.

The goal of leadership is not to be indispensable. The goal is to build something that thrives without you. When done right, positive results grow exponentially.

How to Become a River

Becoming a river does not happen by accident. It requires intentionality. Here are a few practical ways leaders can become rivers.

1. **Whenever possible, share want-to-know information.**
   Look for opportunities to update the team on the broader areas of the business.
2. **Explain decisions, not just outcomes.**
   Walk the team through how you arrived at conclusions. Teach the thinking process.
3. **Invite others into problem-solving early.**
   Don't wait until you have the answer. Let others wrestle with the problem alongside you.
4. **Document lessons learned.**
   Capture insights, so they outlive individuals.
5. **Share context proactively.**
   Don't wait for questions. Anticipate what people are wondering.
6. **Develop successors on purpose.**
   Measure success not by how needed you are, but by how capable your team becomes.

The strongest leaders are rivers, not reservoirs.

They share context generously, and they develop other people intentionally. They view leadership not as control, but as responsibility. In the long run, organizations do not rise because of what leaders know. Leaders who are reservoirs rise because of what they **invest in their teams**. We encourage you to have the mindset of a river, not a reservoir.

Chapter 15 Summary

- Avoid the trap of secrecy; most information is not confidential.
- The best leaders ensure their teams have all the information they need to know, and as much as they want to know as possible.
- Teams are energized by feeling informed, driving better results.
- Leaders who are reservoirs create dependency, while leaders who are rivers build capable teams.
- Becoming a river requires intentionality.

Conclusion

Over the past two decades, the success of Correct Craft has changed countless lives for the better, all around the world. That success did not happen by accident. It was driven by a set of intentional mindsets. Ways of thinking about leadership, people, and purpose that shaped how our team made decisions and showed up every day. Those mindsets are what we have shared in this book.

That is why this book matters. Success creates a platform, and we believe that platform carries responsibility. Because Correct Craft has been successful, we have been able to serve others; our neighbors, customers, employees, vendors, dealers, and communities across the globe.

When business is guided by the right thinking, it can become a force for good.

This book was written at a meaningful moment in Correct Craft's history. For the first time in twenty years, the company is transitioning Chief Executive Officers. With the average CEO tenure lasting roughly five years, we understand the significance of this change, especially following two decades of consistent leadership. Both Bill, the outgoing CEO, and Zach, the incoming CEO, are deeply committed to a successful transition.

One important part of that handoff is preserving what has worked. We do not want to lose the thinking that helped our team succeed. By memorializing these mindsets in this book, we expect to equip our team with a lasting set of tools that will continue to guide decisions, behaviors, and leadership long into the future.

Bill and Zach have used these tools for years. We know they work. We are certain Correct Craft will continue to benefit from them.

But the impact of this book is not limited to Correct Craft.

Any leader who reads these pages, including you, can apply these same tools. We hope that you, wherever you are in your leadership journey, will use them to achieve success in your own organization and then use that success to build a platform that inspires your team and serves others in meaningful ways, both in your community and around the world.

And it all starts with how we think.

Mindset matters.

Appendix Recommended Reading

Leadership & Management

- *Making Life Better* — Bill Yeargin
- *Education of a CEO* — Bill Yeargin
- *The Advantage* — Patrick Lencioni
- *The Truth About Employee Engagement* — Patrick Lencioni
- *The Heart of Leadership* — Mark Miller
- *8 Paradoxes of Great Leadership* — Tim Elmore
- *The Secret of Teams* — Mark Miller
- *Five Dysfunctions of a Team* — Patrick Lencioni
- *Four Stages of Psychological Safety* — Timothy R. Clark
- *Good to Great* — Jim Collins
- *Built to Last* — Jim Collins
- *Excellence Wins* — Horst Schulze
- *Lead From the Future* — Josh Suskewicz & Mark Johnson
- *Derailed* — Tim Irwin
- *Get Off the X* — Michele Rigby Assad
- *A Message to Garcia* — Elbert Hubbard

Personal Growth & Self-Development

- *Atomic Habits* — James Clear
- *Seven Habits of Highly Effective People* — Stephen Covey

- *Mindset* — Carol Dweck
- *13 Things Mentally Strong People Don't Do* — Amy Morin
- *Psycho-Cybernetics* — Maxwell Maltz
- *Learned Optimism* — Martin Seligman
- *This Time Is Different* — Carmen Reinhart & Kenneth Rogoff
- *Being Wrong* — Kathryn Schulz
- *Thinking in Bets* — Annie Duke
- *The Traveler's Gift* — Andy Andrews

Faith, Values & Purpose

- *Faith Leap* — Bill Yeargin
- *The Purpose Driven Life* — Rick Warren
- *Unoffendable* — Brant Hansen
- *Communication for a Change* — Andy Stanley & Lane Jones
- *Pilgrim's Progress* — John Bunyan

Organizational Culture, Teams & Relationships

- *The Power of the Other* — Henry Cloud
- *Necessary Endings* — Henry Cloud
- *5 Languages of People in the Workplace* — Gary Chapman
- *Energy Bus* — Jon Gordon
- *Delivering Happiness* — Tony Hsieh

Strategy, Business Thinking & Innovation

- *Start With Why* — Simon Sinek
- *Measure What Matters* — John Doerr
- *The Halo Effect* — Phil Rosenzweig
- *Innovator's Dilemma* — Clayton Christensen
- *How to Fly a Horse* — Kevin Ashton
- *The Catalyst* — Jonah Berger
- *The Power of Moments* — Chip & Dan Heath

- *Contagious* — Jonah Berger
- *Economics of Higher Purpose* — Robert Quinn

Negotiation, Communication & Influence

- *How to Win Friends and Influence People* — Dale Carnegie
- *Never Split the Difference* — Chris Voss & Tahl Raz
- *Negotiation Genius* — Deepak Malhotra & Max H. Bazerman
- *Who Not How* — Dan Sullivan

Lean, Operations & Continuous Improvement

- *2 Second Lean* — Paul Akers
- *Lean Thinking* — James P. Womack & Daniel T. Jones
- *Lean Six Sigma for Dummies* — John Morgan & Martin Brenig-Jones

Travel, Reflection & Life Perspective

- *Education of a Traveler* — Bill Yeargin
- *Blue Mind* — Wallace J. Nichols

About the Authors

Bill Yeargin

Bill Yeargin has served as the CEO of Correct Craft for twenty years. Under Bill's leadership, Correct Craft won all their industry's major awards and developed a unique culture of "Making Life Better."

A passionate lifelong learner, Bill earned an MBA and completed post-graduate education at Harvard, Stanford, MIT, and the London School of Economics. He has served both the Obama and Trump administrations on cabinet-level advisory councils. *Florida Trend* magazine recognized Bill as one of "Florida's Most Influential Business Leaders."

Bill has been published hundreds of times. He has authored nine books and is a sought-after conference speaker. He and his wife, Leigh, have two daughters, Erin (married to Ben) and Amanda, along with a beautiful granddaughter, Rosie.

Zach Hutcheson

Zach Hutcheson has been named Chief Executive Officer of Correct Craft, effective April 2026. Prior to being named CEO, Zach served as Chief Financial Officer. As CFO, he was responsible for finance, data analytics, and information technology, while also overseeing vertical integration and innovation initiatives across the business.

A committed learner, Zach earned a master's degree in accounting and is a Certified Lean Six Sigma Black Belt. In addition, he has completed post-graduate education at Harvard, Stanford, University of Pennsylvania, and University of Chicago's Booth School of Business.

Zach and his wife, Christine, enjoy spending time on the water with their two boys, George and Parker.

www.ingramcontent.com/pod-product-compliance
Lightning Source LLC
Chambersburg PA
CBHW070700190326
41458CB00046B/6804/J